MW01173986

Godly Marriage

For

Married and Engaged Couples

I am my beloved's; my beloved is Mine.
Song of Solomon 6:3

Diane M. Czekala

Edited by
Michael Czekala, Penny Eldred,
Carol Ossenfort and Alice Blackwelder

Published by Restore the Glory Ministries, Inc.

Copyright © 2009, 2010
Published by Restore the Glory Ministries, Inc.

1. Marriage/relationship 2. Healing 3. Christian Life
4. Family 5. Self Help 6. Religion 7.Prayer 8. Deliverance

All rights reserved. No part of this book shall be reproduced or
transmitted in any form or by any means, electronic, mechanical,
magnetic, photographic including photocopying, recording or by
any information storage and retrieval system, without prior written
permission of the author. No liability is assumed with respect to
the use of the information contained in this book.

Used by Permission
New International Version (NIV) © 1984 by Zondervan
Publishing House

New Living Translation (NLT) ©1996, 2004 Tyndale
Charitable Trust

English Standard Version (ESV) ©2001 Crossway
Bibles Good News Publishers

This Book is
Lovingly Dedicated to:

God the Father, God the Son and God the Holy Spirit

My husband,
Michael

My daughter and son in law,
Tania & Christopher

My daughter,
April

And to my son,
Jesse

I also dedicate this book to my grandchildren,
Kevin, Finten, and Avrie Jade

Thanks for believing in me, encouraging me,
and praying me through the hard times.
Rev. Trudy Daley

Special Thanks to my husband
for all his support and help in
pre-editing this book.
Mike

Special Thanks for all your hard work,

Alice Blackwelder

Contents

Prayers for Inner Healing and Deliverance

Introduction

The inspiration for this book came after young women began asking me to give them marriage advice. I realized I needed to give this some careful thought so I could give them good, sound Godly advice. I thought, "Why are they asking *me* for advice?" As I thought and prayed about it, it occurred to me, "Why not?" I have been married for thirty-five years. I have gained wisdom and spiritual strength through my trials and blessings from my relationship commitment. I believe when God gives us insight and wisdom, it is not only for our own growth but to be shared with others so they too can benefit as well. I asked the Lord for help and direction, and He started quickly downloading advice and wisdom to me. Throughout my day, I had to run to grab a pen and paper on a regular basis to write the things that were flowing before I forgot what He was telling me. I might add, it had a tremendous impact on my own marriage in a wonderful way.

"Older women must train up the younger women to love their husbands and their children, to live wisely and be pure, to work in their homes, to do good, and to be submissive to their husbands. Then they will not bring shame on the word of God." Titus 2:4-5 New Living Translation (NLT).

This book is a collection of advice, scripture, wisdom and good sound teaching for a successful godly marriage. We are living in a time when divorce is the answer to the difficulties of marriage. We are living in a culture where people discard their relationships and even their unborn babies when it is inconvenient or challenging to them. Often people think they are with the wrong person or made a mistake. We need to realize we can get through the hard times and we will be forever blessed when we do. With God we can get through hard times. What seems right to us is not always right to God. Isaiah 55:8 states, "My thoughts are nothing like your thoughts, says the Lord. And my ways are far beyond anything you could imagine. Just as the heavens are higher than the earth, so my ways are higher than your ways and my thoughts higher than your thoughts."

I include prayers for inner healing and breaking curses. Please feel free to highlight these or anything for future reference. They can be prayed as you read the book or years down the road when you recognize issues arising in your life.

You might wonder, what is a curse? Let me explain beforehand so that you may better understand the prayers. A curse is an unseen force that influences our lives in a negative way. Curses come as a result of living in opposition to God and His perfect plan for our lives. I will explain with scriptures to back it that God is not standing and waiting to punish us. Quite the opposite, God is waiting and always passionately pursuing us, drawing us to Him out of love. Teacher, author, and prophet, John Sandford[1], teaches that in the beginning when God created the Universe, different laws were set in the fabric of creation. Like gravity, what goes up must come down. God does not stand and command what goes up to come down; it just happens because it is in the laws of creation itself.

When we sin, there are natural consequences that happen because we have stepped outside of His boundaries of protection. There are consequences to these actions. These consequences can be carried down through the generations, meaning something that affects us could be because of a sin of ours or of one of

8

our ancestors. There is scripture to back this. For example, NIV Exodus 34:7 "Yet He does not leave the guilty unpunished; he punishes the children and their children for the sin of the fathers to the third and fourth generation." This means that what we do greatly affects our children, our grandchildren and future generations.

Our own sinful actions can cause a curse to come against us. People can talk and speak negatively with hatred to us or about us, or place a curse on us in anger, intentionally or in ignorance. We or our ancestors may have participated in witchcraft, satanism or the occult which can also bring a curse on us. There are many things in today's culture that appear to be acceptable in our daily life but according to the Bible are not right or acceptable to God. You may have participated in some of these and cursed yourself without even knowing it.

Here is a partial list of things that would bring a curse:
- Gossiping
- Astrology
- Horoscopes
- Astral projection
- Witchcraft or WICCA, Wiccan – white magic, Black magic or any color magic
- Casting spells
- Channeling
- Mediums or any calling of the dead
- Psychics
- Tarot cards reading
- Séances
- Ouija boards
- Reading of tea leaves
- Divination of any form

- Transcendental meditation
- Automatic writing
- Amulets
- Voodoo – white or black
- Blood Covenants
- Numerology (this does not include biblical numbers)
- New Age
- Eastern Religions
- Cults
- Spiritualism
- Kabala
- the use of drugs to alter our senses or for spiritual trips and journeys
- Taking vows and oaths in groups, such as joining fraternities and secret societies like the Masons, Knights of Columbus, Moose, and Elks Clubs.

The vows made during initiation rights invoke serious curses that affect not only us, but our family and future generations. The higher we go in the secret societies, the more vows and their curses come against our generational line. There are consequences to all these and many more.

Other possibilities for bringing on curses could include:
- Having an abortion
- Broken covenants such as divorce
- Adultery
- Premarital sex
- Prostitution
- Homosexuality and any other sexual perverse act that takes us outside the boundaries of God's protection.

- Bitterness
- Sexual perversion
- Rebellion
- Lust
- Selfishness

Leviticus, chapters 17-19 lists many of the things we need to stay away from to keep ourselves clean. That's why God gave us the Ten Commandments for our protection. Why do parents make rules for their children? For their protection. Why do we have traffic laws or social laws? For our protection. God says in the Bible that we defile ourselves by practicing or doing any of these things. He wants us holy so things will go well with us. He wants us to stay within His boundary of protection so we are safe from harm and He can draw near to us. Once we step outside that boundary, we are no longer protected by His grace and are in the territory of the enemy.

Deuteronomy chapter 28 contains a lot of verses and useful guidelines on curses. I encourage you to read it in its entirety. Verse 1 begins by saying, "If you fully obey the Lord your God and carefully keep all His commands that I am giving you today, the Lord your God will set you high above all the nations of the world. You will experience all these blessings if you obey the Lord your God."

For the next thirteen verses God explains all the beautiful, wonderful blessings of being obedient and staying within His boundaries of protection. Verse 15 begins the curses for disobedience: "But if you refuse to listen to the Lord your God and do not obey all the commands and decrees I am giving you today, all these curses will come and overwhelm you." Jeremiah

32:18 says, "You show unfailing love to thousands, but you also bring the consequences of one generation's sin upon the next."

I also include prayers for breaking curses because in marriage we reap the sinful things we have sown in the past, and these affect our marriage. These prayers will help to purify ourselves and this affects our marriage and family.

Simple prayers have great power and will break the power of sin and darkness that may come upon us and hinder our lives and relationships. Not every prayer will pertain to you but many will.

I want to give you wisdom and knowledge. Proverbs 4:7 says, "Getting wisdom is the wisest thing you can do!" Hosea 4:6 states, "My people perish for lack of knowledge." To the best of my ability, I want to share what I feel will help strengthen a marriage that is new or old. I share this not only out of my own experience but through training and experience ministering to others with what I have seen that helped to set people free.

My prayer is that you will not be in denial and that you would be willing to change, stretch and grow as a husband or a wife. This book is helpful for an engaged couple, those recently married or those who have been married for many years. Keep it and reread it in a few years.

It is my hope that you will find not just helpful tips for marriage, but that you will be healed and delivered through applying the knowledge in this book to your personal life. A good marriage does not always come naturally or easily, but we must be open to search our hearts, be open to changing ourselves to be a better husband or a better wife. Read this together, have discussions and pray together throughout this book, whether you are engaged or married many years.

God bless you as you become cleansed through the Name of Jesus, and as you do this you will draw near to the Living God, our Father.

1

Till Death Do Us Part

Marriage is our life's journey, to and with the Lord. It is a wonderful way of life, a gift from God. Our spouse is God's gift to us to walk with us through this journey.

Our relationship should enhance our physical, mental and spiritual life. Divorce is much too popular these days and has even become an epidemic. There are key ways to keep our marriage not only strong but sweet, holy and enjoyable. Even the best marriages can run into rough roads or roadblocks which can shake what seemed unshakable. We need to allow God to be number one in our lives and stay in the center of our marriage and family. God will give us the grace we need to not only save our marriage in difficult times but to also have a happier and healthier marriage. This means a happier and healthier life.

Many times one may love a person but have a check in his or her spirit that something is just not right. When it is right, you know that you know...this is the right person. Don't marry someone when you have that check in your spirit. Maybe you cannot put your finger on it, but you just know something is not right. Maybe you are waiting for that someone to change or grow up emotionally. Maybe you think you can change them. That check in your spirit could be God communicating to you, causing you to look deeper into the relationship. You've got to have that godly assurance.

If you find many warning you it is not right or that you're moving too quickly, take to heart the wisdom and hold off marrying. They may be seeing something you don't; seek God and pray about it. If there is a problem before marriage, it is guaranteed it will grow larger during the marriage. Marriage does not solve problems.

If you have had a bad experience in your choices before, you may not trust your judgment. You may need healing and need to forgive yourself for choosing wrongly. You will need to break the unhealthy, ungodly soul ties between you and the past relationship(s), especially if it was an engagement or marriage. I have to admit, I believe some can make mistakes and marry the wrong person. In this case it is bad from the get-go and is very short lived. It is hard to save a marriage that was never good from the start, as when a couple did not reveal their true identities to the other until they trapped the other. I know God does save marriages and with God all things are possible, but some of these possibly were never meant to be.

In Biblical times, an engagement was as binding as a marriage; they were considered married. It was a promise to marry; if it was broken, it was a broken promise. You need to forgive the other and yourself for breaking the covenant, and forgive yourself for choosing wrongly. Also break the ungodly bond that still holds the two of you together. Ask the Lord to break any spiritual connection between the two of you.

It may be difficult to move on to marry another if those ungodly bonds still hold you back, or you now have a lack of trust in yourself. For example, forgive yourself or them for breaking the engagement, abandoning you on your wedding day, or leaving you while married, etc... This should help heal your heart and help you trust yourself again, if this is the case.

You need that assurance from God that this is the right person. Don't marry just because someone is there, or marry just to be married. Don't think you can change people; either they are right for you or they are not. No one is perfect and flawless, but the question is are they the one for you? If you are reading this and you have not found someone, ask God to help you find the one He has already chosen for you.

Ask yourself this question, do I want to spend the rest of my life with this person? What issues keep you from wanting this? Get to the heart of the problem. Discuss it with close, mature friends. There are good engagement books that examine many subjects. They encourage you to share your feelings and thoughts about each subject to really get to know each other and find out if you are truly compatible.

Be honest in answering the questions in these types of books or questionnaires in premarital counseling sessions; you are only hurting yourself if you don't answer them honestly. It is healthy and even fun to get to know your loved one better. Don't be afraid to break it off if you are not compatible; it hurts now, but not as much as it would if you follow through anyhow and marry the wrong person. There are some exercises in the back of this book for engaged as well as married couples that are helpful. Don't misrepresent yourself by answering what the other person wants to hear. You answer honestly by who you are.

Many times people marry for the wrong reasons and those reasons are not good or firm enough to hold a marriage together. One example may be loneliness.

Some marry the wrong people because they do not want to be alone. If you do not love someone with your whole heart and they are your best friend, think again. Also many times a couple will marry because of a pregnancy or stay together because of the children. If it is not solid enough on it's own it will be difficult to keep it together.

There is the time when the children grow up and move out and leave the parents alone again as they started. If there is not a solid foundation there can be a divorce after 20 years.

On the other hand empty nest can be a wonderful time in life when the couple feels like newlyweds again without the responsibilities of raising children. They often begin doing things they've wanted to do like traveling and enjoying retirement life together. I remember looking back on my parents when they went into retirement and senior living and they were like teenagers. Always doing something or going some place. I said, "I want to be like them when I get there."

When a man or woman leaves his/her parents, there is still a bond with the parents, but it changes so we can become one with, and have the stronger bond with, our husband or wife. We no longer answer to our parents but to our spouse. If the attachment to a parent remains too strong in an unhealthy way, somehow this may get in the way of the bonding with the new spouse and in the marriage itself.

"For this reason a man will leave his father and mother and be united to his wife, and they will become one flesh." Gen 2:24. Your wife or husband must come first, and if your parents don't understand things you may do, or the way you choose to raise your family, remember, your wife or husband and family comes

18

first. Don't judge your parents if they don't understand you; love them where they are and forgive them.

Sometimes parents love a child so much that they have a difficult time backing off and letting go, and letting their son or daughter bond fully with the spouse. This can hinder the marriage relationship. Perhaps they have a need or desire to have their hands in their children's lives too much. This can be a problem if ties are too tight for comfort, especially when manipulation and control are involved. This can happen in a young couple and even with an older couple if allowed to continue.

- Are either of your parents the subject of argument in your relationship?
- Do you feel guilty or have a hard time making a decision if it contradicts the ideals of your parent's, even when you know it is right for you and your spouse?
- Do you feel a force making it difficult?

These issues can be prayed through and "ungodly" soul ties between the child and parent can be broken by a simple spoken prayer. Only the "ungodly," insecure, unhealthy ties are broken. The right and godly bond remains.

You can do this with any unhealthy relationship. You can ask yourself some questions.
- Do you feel in bondage to or by a person?
- Does someone else manipulate you?
- Are you manipulating a person, spouse, son, daughter, or parent?
- Do you feel controlled or dominated by someone?
- Have you bound yourself to another with a

promise, vow or blood covenant?

No person, your husband or wife, parent or in-law, neighbor, co-worker, boss, or friend should be doing any of these things to you. It is wrong. It is possible the offending person is not even aware of what they are doing to the other.

In a marriage relationship, both should be properly submitted to one another. There should not be any unfaithfulness, control over one another, or unhealthy aggressive dominance. This will cause the other to be weak, defeated, manipulated and controlled. These are not healthy, godly attributes. There should also be no holding back one's affections from the other.

Check yourself; do you feel a desire to control or manipulate another in your family, among your friends or people in general? This can happen in different ways. All of these things cause pain, weakness, powerlessness and the feeling of being crippled or imprisoned. Not only can a husband or wife be this way to each other but to their children. Children can also do it to parents. If you see this starting, you need to carefully mold the strong-willed child without breaking his or her spirit. Teenagers can especially overrule parents in rebelliousness, manipulation, and control. Children and teens can manipulate with anger and violence, as can adults.

Prayer for Breaking Unhealthy Soul Ties

Pray the prayers out loud to God.

I break all ungodly soul ties between myself and my mother and father (or whoever it may be) in Jesus' Name. Tie all loose ties to You, Lord. I break all ungodly manipulation and control in Jesus' Name. I forgive my (mother/father/person). I renounce all generational spirits that may be causing this to happen, in Jesus' Name. I break all the assignments of the enemy off of my relationship with my mother and father or _____ in Jesus' Name. Bless and restore our relationship to the way You would have it be, Lord. I forgive them for holding on too tightly and not wanting to let go. Set me free in the Mighty Name of Jesus, Amen. Lord restore healthy bonds with my spouse, and cover that bond with the Precious Blood of Jesus, in Jesus Name. Amen.

Prayer if you are the parent holding on too tightly to a grown child

Lord, I repent for holding onto my children too tightly. I repent for selfishly manipulating or controlling them and their spouses in any ungodly way. Help me to let go so they can bond properly with their spouse. Cut the ungodly soul ties I have with _____. (Name children, grandchildren, or person, each separately out loud.) **Restore good Godly ties between us. Bind all lose ties to You, Lord. Bond_____properly with their husband/wife. I repent for getting between them. I'm sorry for not trusting You, Lord. I entrust them to you Lord. Remove any obstacles I may have put between them. Cover their marriage with the Precious Blood of Jesus. I renounce all generational spirits that may be manipulating me and my family, in Jesus' Name I pray, Amen.** This type of prayer can be done for anyone it pertains to, not just family.

This also applies to a husband and a wife; there should be a healthy bond between them. One should not be holding on too tightly to the other out of insecurities. There should be a healthy secure love.

This bond is like a cord attached from one to the other person with whom we have relationship. It cannot be seen by the natural eye because it is a spiritual cord. I have seen these cords, by the Holy Spirit, while ministering to people. I have seen little demons sitting on these cords, while I was praying for people with damaged relationships and marriages. We must be assured that we have authority and can easily send the enemy away, canceling their assignments in Jesus' Name.

I have seen a husband or wife, or both, holding onto the cord[2] with their hand. This means he or she is holding too tightly onto the other out of insecurities and possessiveness. In a marriage, this can cause one spouse to feel bound up with a lack of freedom. It is also possible that both can be holding on too tightly. We want our relationships to be healthy ones. If you feel this is you, you can pray this simple prayer. Pray whenever you feel the need arise.

Simple prayer to end the attack of the enemy against your marriage

Lord, I repent for holding onto my spouse or fiancé too tightly out of my own insecurities. Make my relationship right and healthy, in Jesus' Name. (Have spouse forgive you audibly.) In Jesus' Name, I bind up every demon coming against and tampering with my marriage relationship and bond, in Jesus' Name. I cancel the assignments of the enemy against my spouse and me, and off my

marriage and family. I break all witchcraft off my household, off my family and off my marriage in the Name of Jesus. Lord, strengthen and bless the bonds of our marriage in the Name of Jesus. Lord, cover our marriage bond with the precious blood of Jesus, in Jesus' Name, Amen.

Sometimes the enemy will put thoughts in one's head about past relationships; that what you had was better than what you have now, creating a false love and false memory, or false hope and distraction. Do not hold these thoughts and entertain them as if they were true. Don't forget the bad that caused the relationship to end. If it were true, you would be married to that person now. There was a valid reason why you broke up with him or her. If you were never actually with the person, there is a valid reason why you weren't, and it is all fantasy.

The enemy would whisper in our ears for these ideas to come against our marriage; sometimes it is our flesh, but it will cause you pain and harm the marriage, or cause you to fall into an adulterous relationship. It is a fantasy which can be sin. Sometimes our flesh is weak, and we can fall into this during hard times. Jesus said if we even think it in our thoughts we have already committed adultery. As soon as a bad idea comes in your mind, stop it right there.

Jesus, too, was tempted in the desert, and he heard the voice of what the enemy was saying. He did not sin by hearing the devil speak. He came against it by the Word. Often people think they have sinned because a sinful thought has entered their mind. No, it is what you do with it at that point. Jesus was tempted. Temptation is not sin, because Jesus was without sin.

You must resist, or it will get worse. Refuse and resist. Do not accept the thoughts. Ask the Lord to break the unhealthy bonds of love between you and this person. Often these thoughts come from having an ungodly soul tie with someone. We need to break all ungodly soul ties with this person. Repent for any ungodly sex outside of marriage. Repent for living with them; this causes bonds. Break the bonds from living with this person. If this is an ex-spouse, pray to break the ungodly soul ties with him/her. Sometimes if you took drugs with a person, there is an ungodly tie. Repent and pray to break it, always in Jesus' Name.

Prayers to Break Unhealthy Bonds with Past Relationships

Lord, I ask you to break all false love, false hope and all false fantasies, and I repent for sinning by putting my heart into these. (If any of these is the case, or if there is something the Lord shows you about the past relationship(s) not listed, pray appropriately as the Holy Spirit leads.) **If you fell and entertained these thoughts, repent for yearning for another person in fantasy. I also renounce any spirits connected to this person or connected to me from any of my ancestors that may be holding me to this person_____. Ask the Lord to restore your marriage to where it should be, in Jesus' Mighty Name. Lord break all these ungodly soul ties and cover them with the Precious Blood of Jesus. Lord I also ask that you cover and seal my godly tie and godly bond with my spouse with Your Precious Blood, Jesus. In Jesus Name I pray.**

You may also break the ungodly ties to worldly, dark or demonic music. Maybe music we listened to when we were with an old relationship still holds us to the person in some way or a spirit attached to the music. Many times the enemy can work through music by implanting the spirit of fear, rebellion, lust, violence, or ties to the world of darkness. This is especially true when accompanied with the use of drugs, and all types of perversion.

Again, just pray to break the ungodly ties with all such music. Command and Renounce every demon that attached to you through music, in Jesus' Name. Amen. Go to the root, the entry point if you remember. Repent, Ask the Lord to break the power of darkness over you from this act. Command the enemy out, in Jesus' Name. (this is best done with a Spirit filled person. They can command the enemy out as well.)

In the same way as when we listen to godly, anointed music we are filled with God's peace, and Presence. Through this we can even touch God and seem to translate to heaven. So is it with ungodly music we can be filled with ungodly things and be filled with the presence of demons and darkness.

Often music seems harmless, even good and enjoyable. It does not only have to be in the form of hard rock music which seems most common. The enemy is trickier than that. My husband was listening to the radio to soft worshipful-like music which he said, "It was the most beautiful music I've ever heard." When he began to listen closer they were worshiping satan. He was shocked and appalled. Also, what spirit in the person singing comes across through music. Were the people full of sinfulness, on drugs, full of violence, and rebellion during the time when writing, singing, and performing such music?

Next, a husband or wife should not be too distant, acting as if there is no bond at all. If one spouse is too distant emotionally, it may cause insecurities in the other. Maybe a spouse never wants to touch, hug or hold; this can be painful to the other, especially if he or she is a person needing touch as most people do. We all need healthy touches. Those who cannot hug or be close to their spouse may be this way because they weren't touched affectionately enough, or at all, as children. Also some may have been touched inappropriately by the same or opposite sex, or sexually abused in a greater way. This can be healed when gone back to the time and deal with issues attached at that time.

When parents, grandparents, or even foster parents, etc. are unaffectionate; it is carried down throughout the generations and it is taught or caught whether you desired it or not. That does not make it right. You need to forgive the parent for not properly fulfilling your needs. I have seen some adults still trying to get a parent's love and approval without succeeding because the parent had never received it, and still does not know how to give it. It leaves the child, even as an adult, hungry for the love and approval he/she never received.

This may have caused you to judge the parent consciously or unconsciously. Either way, you or your spouse may need to stretch yourself and change in order to care for the affectionate needs of the other. This will make for a happy, healthy relationship. Just as there was affectionate touching and talking before marriage, this needs to continue throughout the marriage. I will cover sexual abuse prayers later in this book.

Prayer for Lack of Affection

Lord, help me to be able to receive affection. Help me to want affection and want to give affection to my husband/wife.

Lord, I ask that you restore in me affection, affectionate touch and the love I did not receive as an infant and child growing up. Sometimes I had a hard time pleasing my parents and felt I had to prove myself, or that I had to work for their love and acceptance. I repent for judging them for this, and I forgive my parents. I also repent for judging their marriage relationship. I forgive them all their sins while I was yet in the womb and while I was growing up. I know You were always with me, even in the hard times and held me each time I needed it.

If for some reason I did not bond, cleave or join with my (wife) or (husband) appropriately, I ask, Lord, join me with my spouse by the Precious Blood of Jesus. Help me to love my (wife) (husband) like you do and teach me how to love. Teach me how You would have me love _____. Give me Your love and affection for my spouse. I cannot do it without you; help me to love her/him properly to fulfill his/her needs. Stop the judgments from coming back on me, in Jesus' Name. If I in any way built a wall of protection to deal with this, please break down that wall. If I hardened myself, please soften my heart Lord. I repent for doing this. If I stuffed my hurt feelings down inside as a child, please release them now; take them all and heal me, in Jesus' Name. Thank you Lord, Amen. It is good for the spouse to lay hands on the other while they are praying this prayer and agree with you in prayer

Take some time and ask the Lord to speak to you about what He thinks about the situations you are praying about. What does He have to say about them?

When my children were babies, I began praying for their future spouses. I knew their future spouses were young as well. I prayed for them where they were.

Prayer for Children's Future Spouses:

God protect them and make Yourself known to them right now and throughout their lives. Protect them from the schemes of the enemy. Cancel all the assignments of the enemy off their lives, in Jesus' Name. Lord, prepare them for each other through their lives. Cause them to be all they should be, in Jesus' Name. Amen.

As my children got older and when I saw them in unhealthy relationships, I prayed to break the power of the enemy against them. I prayed God's will for their lives. I prayed against the enemy in any way trying to prevent them from meeting God's chosen one for them. I prayed to break that plan and power of the enemy off their lives, in Jesus Name.

Do not pray controlling prayers. Prayers should never be *my* will but *God's* will for them. This is very important, because once we pray "our" will, it becomes witchcraft. I have felt people's prayers pushing me in a certain direction and when it is not God's direction, it is uncomfortable and sometimes painful. God knows; He created just the right person for each of us.

Often as parents who are in the Lord, we may have good discernment and see the truth. The problem is that no one is 100% accurate all of the time, and we may not always know the truth and must be very careful.

My parents did not like my husband at all; not until we became engaged, then they loved him. They didn't know him. They didn't know the good I saw in him. He also was not all God had created him to be yet. He was still a work in progress, just as we both were and still are. They saw his long hair, and that was a stumbling block to them. On the other side, his father did not care for me, but as time passed we both had a love and respect for each other. I did not want to make this mistake, so I just prayed that they would be in God's will and tried to see my children's boyfriends or girlfriends as God saw them.

Many times we are very compatible with our husband or wife, but the plan of the enemy gets in the way to tamper with our compatibility. Marriage is not always easy. It just needs to be worked through during difficult times. How are we going to get through this, is the question? Both need to make an effort to keep the marriage going. Often prayer will break the powers against us; sometimes prayer and fasting. Ephesians 6:12 says, "For we are not fighting against flesh and blood enemies, but against evil rulers and authorities of the unseen world, against mighty powers in this dark world, and against evil spirits in the heavenly places."

When we are under attack, we are no longer alone so we not only pray for our needs but we need to pray for our spouse on a regular basis. Intercession should be a part of EVERY Christian's life. We need to pray for our spouse and hold him/her up, especially when we see them going through a trying time. When we have children, we need to pray for our children. I wore the knees off my pants praying for my children and my husband.

I was so impressed that when my daughter was not even married yet God gave her fiancé a dream. The dream showed him that she needed prayer, and he actually interceded in the dream for her and woke up praying for her. He was praying for her before they even became husband and wife. He was already a praying husband. We need to hold each other up in prayer. Not only pray *with* each other but pray *for* each other. Not our will but God's will.

We need to understand that our spouse is not the enemy when things go wrong; it is the enemy fighting against our marriage, and he is out to kill, steal and destroy. I am going to repeat that; it is worth repeating. We need to remember that it is not our spouse who is the enemy when things are not right; it is the devil. He does this by coming against one or both of the individuals, specifically the mind. The enemy also can use your young children or teens to come against you as well. Marriage is so precious to our Lord that the enemy loves to come against it.

Think about it; family is the nurturing womb for our children. If marriage is broken, then family is broken apart and young minds, hearts and spirits are broken. The percentage of divorce is almost as high for Christians as it is for unbelievers. We have strategy and prayer! My hope is that when trouble comes, you can look back and use the prayers in this book to help you. This is not just a read it once book. Allow it to give you strategy against the enemy in your life.

Often times, the enemy is planted to literally whisper negative words in our ears. It is planted in our thoughts as if it were coming from our own mind. Now don't get me wrong here. I am not giving any glory to satan, but what I am doing is exposing the tricks of the enemy so you'll be that much wiser to come against the liar. When you hear a negative word in your head, just bind the enemy, close his mouth and send him off in the Name of Jesus. Don't make his words your own. Don't own them! And just praise the Lord. It is our duty to know how the enemy works to protect not only ourselves but others who are in need. Jesus speaks many times about the devil in the scriptures, because we need to know how the enemy works to have victory over him. Soldiers are trained to know the schemes of their enemies. We, too, are better off when we know and are prepared for his tricks.

"Fix your thoughts on what is true and honorable and right, and pure and lovely and admirable. Think about things that are excellent and worthy of praise. Keep putting into practice all you have learned and received from me – everything you learned from me and saw me doing. Then the God of peace will be with you." Philippians 4:8.

Look at that first word, fix. We must fix our eyes and thoughts on what is good. When the enemy comes, it is a fight and we must intentionally set our attention in the right direction. "Resist the enemy and he will flee from you." James 4:7. The enemy can try to come and cause havoc in your family and your home. If you would recognize what is happening, you could use the authority given to us by God and pray against it, in Jesus' Name. We have power over the devil in the Name of Jesus. He has given us authority. The enemy would have you believe you don't have the authority; he is a liar.

We need to daily put on the full Armor of God; just say every morning, "**Lord, I put on the full Armor of God and cover myself with the Precious Blood of Jesus, in the Name of the Father, Son and Holy Spirit. Thank you Lord, Amen.**"

Women, when we feel cranky because of our hormonal status, we still need to press in and fix our thoughts on what is good. Hormones are no excuse for sin and spewing all over our man because we "feel" like it. You will fail at times, but it is a time we need to consciously work harder at overcoming and not acting on those negative feelings.

Many women can have wacky hormones from Pre-menstrual Syndrome (PMS), menstruation side effects, pre-menopause complications and difficulty transitioning into menopause. Women go through a lot. Reading the Word, prayer, worship and soaking in the Lord, is the best medicine for these types of problems. I've been through it all, and this was extremely helpful during severe hormonal times. There is something powerful about soaking in anointed music; it is like a spiritual shower, and it bathes us and washes off the junk. (Also, a natural progesterone crème was extremely helpful in all of the cases.)

When we soak in His Presence, it spiritually tunes us back toward God and His Kingdom rather than the world and its ways, by which we are continually surrounded. Also playing anointed worship music in our homes cleanses the spiritual atmosphere in our homes. It makes a home a more desirable place for godliness and holiness to dwell; a less desirable place for the enemy to dwell. God has used the anointing through music since back in the Old Testament when David played his harp to settle Saul's spirit when the enemy would attack him. David's harp was anointed worship. "Whenever the tormenting spirit from God troubled Saul, David would play the harp. Then Saul would feel better, and the tormenting spirit would go away." (God allowed the tormenting spirit [a curse] because of Saul's sins.) NLT 1 Samuel 16:23.

When we don't pray, worship, go to church, or take Communion regularly, we get tuned-in to the world. We can get tuned in to the world by watching lots of television, listening to secular music, reading secular books. We resonate more with this world than the Kingdom of God. We can become more negative and worldly-minded, but when we pray and soak and read the Bible, we become more like Him, and our husband or wife and children will notice.

The enemy will come in where there is a crack, and hormones gone wacky can be an open door for the enemy if we lose our temper or say and do things unacceptable and hurtful. We need to be accountable to each other. Men, instead of running away or turning your back on her when hormones get wacky, which can be easy, pray instead. Prayer is the best antidote, and what most men don't realize is that as husbands you have authority to calm the storm of confusion and command the hormones to function normally in her body, in Jesus' Name. By acting in love and patience, it comes against the negative that the hormonal imbalance causes.

Prayer for your Wife's Hormonal Imbalance

Lay hands on your wife and pray, I bind the attacks of the enemy. **I Call the peace and calm of God upon you and into you, in Jesus' Name. I command your hormones to normalize. I command all confusion to go, in Jesus' Name.** Encourage her to soak in anointed worship music. Love, be patient and continue to pray.

When PMS gets out of control, it can be scary for young men and women. It is an emotional roller coaster for her and just as scary for the husband.

Neither fully understands what is going on. Confusion can set in, and it is an open door for the enemy to take over.

Not every woman goes through this, but there are many young and older women struggling to get through monthly stresses and sicknesses. Men, you have authority over your wife and family and this makes your prayers extra powerful. The enemy knows this, but unfortunately many men do not. It is easy to take things personal, get upset, and not even think of praying, but now you know and can overcome.

I once heard a man say that his friend actually divorced his wife because of her monthly PMS. He said she turned into a different woman at that time, and he could not take it. I wonder what would have happened had he known to pray for her and give her extra love at those times? What if he had known to break the power of the enemy attacking her, to pray for peace over her mind? This is a sad story. The same goes for women with men. Not much is said about men's hormones, but clearly they have hormones as well and times when we, too, need to do the same for them. This is not a time to be offensive but prayerful, loving and forgiving.

In marriage, we need to be very careful how we handle our emotions, both male and female. We get wrong attitudes with our loved one, and it seems to scar our relationship, especially when one or both are sensitive.

You have heard the saying, we hurt the ones we love? It is true, and it does not need to be that way. As we continue to hurt one another, not caring about the other's feelings, this greatly harms our relationship. There is always hope for healing, and forgiveness is vital. In the most difficult situations, even if you are already separated, trust and love can be restored with God's help.

Guard against holding onto hurtful things, not forgiving, and harboring bitterness in your hearts. This is very dangerous to us and our relationships. Most often when our spouse is acting undesirably, it is because they had a bad day, something has happened or, believe it or not, it is often in reaction to our bad behavior toward them.

Sometimes we cannot control our feelings and lash out and hurt one another. We need an attitude of working things out by discussing things. It does not have to be in anger or a shouting match. There will be differences. We help to balance each other out.

Feelings are responses or reactions to emotions which often erupt now, in the present, because of an incident from our past or our childhood. It may possibly be from a stressful situation or how a parent may have treated us as a child.

When the husband or wife unknowingly acts in a similar way, it triggers those old reactions. The feelings were buried but still alive and now come out. "Whoa! Where did that come from?" There is an OVER reaction that does not fit the situation. "I don't remember seeing him/her act that way when we were dating or courting", you may think. Feelings can also be difficult to communicate.

There is not much difference between feelings and emotions. Some can be negative and some positive. Negative feelings and thoughts can give birth to sin. Feelings can be attitudes and reactions from our past experiences. Many people need to learn to handle their emotions rightly. Many lose control.

Feelings, thoughts, and words have energy and vibration. You can agree when you have come against someone angry and bitter that the feelings flow strongly from them, and you feel the vibration and negative energy strongly against your body. It can even overcome you and catch you, so to speak, on fire of the same negativity. It is like a force which has a ripple effect. You see this play out in your own family and in a greater effect on the world.

Put one very negative person in a workplace or room with others, and he/she seems to overtake the others. It shouldn't be that way, but negative forces are very strong. It is up to us as Christians to be sure to not let negativity, which is a force from the enemy, take us over. "He who is in us is greater than the one who is in the world." 1 John 4:4. This is especially true in our home; we should be peacemakers. This is accomplished by staying strong in prayer, praying in tongues quietly, reading the word daily, taking communion, and soaking in prayer to anointed music, all of which extinguishes the negative powers of the enemy and strengthens our spirit.

Place yourself in powerful worship services with preaching of the Word; all these things work against the negative power against us. God's presence, anointing, and power transform us. We become the positive effect in our home, marriage, family and workplace.

For some reason negativity sticks to our flesh like a magnet. It takes effort and vibrant prayer to come against it. Know that if you are around a lot of negativity you will have to do some extra things to protect yourself. We don't want to pass it on to our family.

By harboring sorrows, bitterness, negativity, unforgiveness, and judgments in our hearts, we allow those things to take us over. We become more bitter and unforgiving, and it can even affect our health. We must forgive and get things out. We cannot shove them down, we must deal with things. When we bury things, they never die but live on deep within us and affect our lives in the future. They seem to make us who we are and alter how we act. If handled properly, by dealing with situations, they don't seem to have that negative impact on us.

We are not perfect people. We are two imperfect people coming together as "one." That means his imperfections become one with mine, and mine with his. We don't know how to deal with these new imperfections. We are two adults with little children inside, meaning something may trigger a wound from childhood and it becomes very real, and he/she feels just as he/she did when it first happened. Because it was not handled properly or dealt with, that child tantrum may come out of a 30 or 40 year old, or whatever age person. It will come out on those closest to us...our husband, wife or children.

It can be something possibly suppressed or hidden in the one being triggered. This person doesn't know why he/she is acting that way. You may even see your spouse acting just like his or her parents. Many times we pick up good and godly traits from our parents, but unfortunately too often it is a parent's negative, sinful reaction that is learned, and the child has judged it; they most likely do not even know they are doing it. Often times when we are in stressful situations, we revert to a childhood state. These are the times our true character is being tested.

We need to be careful to not hurt each other. It is when we don't care that this is most likely to happen. We must recognize when negative reaction is coming out of us; that is an area we may need inner healing in. It can harm the marriage relationship if not dealt with, but we can both pray together to get to the bottom of it. Of course, both parties have to realize this and not be in denial that they're doing anything wrong.

Sometimes it is very hard to see the wrong in ourselves, but much easier to see the faults in our spouse. Many times it is our own negative childish actions or reactions that our spouse is reacting to. Ask God to bring those actions to light, to show you where the root of them is from, and to make it known to you.

John Sandford[3] says there is a root experience or memory of where negative reactions came from and actually began. Let me explain; sinful reactions can be anger, rage, control, drunkenness, abuse, anything negative, hurtful or sinful. Track it back to the memory where the wound and judgment began. Often we have sown judgments against our parents as young children; we reap what we have sown, and it comes right back on us, the very thing we judged. Most of us do not remember doing this since it was done unknowingly and at a young age. It is often not activated until we get married and/or have children.

"Do not be deceived: God cannot be mocked. A man reaps what he sows. The one who sows to please his sinful nature, from that nature will reap destruction. The one who sows to please the spirit, from the Spirit will reap eternal life." NIV Galatians 6:7-8.

"They sow the wind and reap the whirlwind." Hosea 8:7 This means not only do we reap the negative we've sown, but it grows and grows and by the time it gets back to us, it has grown into a monster. **We first need to forgive our parents.**

NIV Deuteronomy 5:16 says, "Honor your father and your mother, as the Lord your God has commanded you, so that you may live long and that it may go well with you in the land the Lord your God is giving you." We must honor our mother and father so it may go well with us. What if we didn't honor them, and we don't remember or didn't even realize we weren't honoring them? We are going to reap what we've sown whether we remember it or not, or whether we like it or not.

Remember also; we must forgive so we may be forgiven. This does not necessarily mean what they did was right or it does not necessarily mean they were wrong; just that we judged an emotion or action and perceived it to be wrong and that very thing will come up in us. Sometimes we remember, and sometimes we don't.

We once knew someone who could not forgive his parents because he thought that by forgiving them, he was saying that what they did was okay. No, forgiving is not saying what they did was right or wrong; forgiving sets us free from the situation. It releases us. Give it to Jesus. Holding something against someone, keeps us bound to them and the incident, and we are open for it to be reaped in our life. Bitterness can set in. We must let go and give it to Jesus, and this sets us free. We all have done this to some degree, but more so when we have been abused. We are more inclined to do the very thing we hated having done to us.

This often happens when you have divorced parents. Children judge the parents and end up in a divorce themselves.

Repent – Forgive – Break Judgments

<u>Prayer to Break Judgments</u>

Have someone agree with you in prayer, if you can.

1. Repent for judging the parent. (grandparent, foster parent, persons, or perhaps even God) **Repent for holding onto resentments. This also could be God, if you are judging; holding unforgiveness or resentments against God. Forgive God if this is you. (Not that He needs our forgiveness; He is Righteous, perfect, and True in all He does. He knows more than we do. Much is hidden from our knowledge)**

There are examples of us holding things against God. Here is one example; if you had a child or parent who died, you may be very upset with God for taking your loved one and you may be consciously or unconsciously holding a grudge. You need to forgive because of your heart, not because of what God did, but because of the judgments and unforgiveness in your heart. Forgiving Him sets you free. You may not even know you have done this.

2. Forgive the parent or person for his/her hurtful actions, reactions and words against you.

3. Repent for judging, unforgiveness, and harboring bitterness through the years. Possibly you need to repent for your sinful reactions.

4. Lord I accept your forgiveness. Have someone verbally forgive you if possible. If not say, I accept your forgiveness. Be led by the Holy Spirit in doing these types of prayers, in Jesus' Name.

When you forgive, it stops the negative sowing and reaping process from coming to pass in your life. You can do it alone or with your spouse. Next, you must pray to stop the process of reaping what you have sown.

5. Repent for any inner vows[4] **you remember making and ask God to break them so that they will not come back upon you.**

These can be many things such as the statements, "I will never be like them." "I don't ever want to have children." "I will never hit my kids." "I don't ever want to be a dad." "I will never work all the time and not spend time with my family when I grow up." Even though they are well meaning, vows are like judgments; we will grow up to do that very thing and possibly worse.

5. Put the cross of Christ and His shed Blood between you and the negative thing coming upon you. Stop the process of the sowing and reaping, in Jesus' Name.

6. Ask God to bless you, to restore healthy emotions, and to build new, healthy, godly habits of emotions, new godly reactions, and standards, in Jesus' Name. Always pray in the Name of Jesus. That is where the power and authority lie, not in ourselves. It is through His Name and His work on the cross that the powers of the enemy are broken, and we are set free.

Philippians 2:9 says, "Therefore, God elevated Him to the place of highest honor and gave Him the Name above all other Names, that at the Name of Jesus every knee should bow, in heaven and on earth and under the earth and every tongue confess that Jesus Christ is Lord, to the glory of God the Father."

"Bear with each other and forgive whatever grievances you may have against one another. Forgive as the Lord forgave you." NIV Colossians 3:13.

As negative things arise on a daily basis, walk in this and pray to God. You will receive healing, becoming the spotless bride of Christ. Catch resentments as soon as they start. Forgotten resentments are buried and get lodged deep in the heart, making them more difficult to find and recognize.

You will see a difference in your marriage. As each individual receives healing, the marriage becomes healthier and stronger too. Not only will your marriage be happier but you will be freer to walk in the things that God has for you.

You will learn through this book how to pray inner healing, deliverance, and breaking generational curses. God will reveal the issues that need to be dealt with. Take it one at a time and down the road you will be more and more healed and whole.

Most issues don't arise until after you're married or your children are born. If you've been married for years and have children, you can easily pick these things out in yourself and your spouse. To obtain the greatest benefit of healing prayers, it is important that you try to find these hidden issues in yourself first.

"Look after each other so that none of you fails to receive the grace of God. Watch out that no poisonous root of bitterness grows up to trouble you, corrupting many." NLT Hebrews 12:15.

Ever hear the saying, "Don't let the sun go down on your anger?" Leaving anger and bitterness inside for too long can cause them to seep deep into our hearts. They are poison to us, those around us and to our marriage. That is actually from the Bible, "Don't sin by letting anger control you. Don't let the sun go down while you are still angry, for anger gives a foothold to the devil." NLT Ephesians 5:26.

Unresolved anger comes up and defiles us, as well as those around us. Unfortunately, it is usually those closest to us. Anger opens the door to the enemy and makes it a welcome environment for him to attack and manipulate our minds, thoughts, emotions, and actions. Make sure you do not hold on to things, but let go and quickly forgive. You, too, will need to be forgiven for many things.

Individual or Group Questions

1. In what areas do I need to forgive my parents?

2. Where have I judged them? List them.

3. What prayer needs do I see right now for my husband, wife or fiancé? Ask the Lord to reveal them to you. List and then pray appropriately.

4. In what areas have I let bitterness set in my heart? Forgive, repent for holding on to things and ask God to take it out of your heart. Accept the Lord's forgiveness.

2

Life

God created everything to be fruitful and to be multiplied. Then God said, "Let the waters swarm with fish and other life. Let the skies be filled with birds of every kind." "So God created great sea creatures and every living thing that scurries and swarms in the water, and every sort of bird – each producing offspring of the same kind. And God saw that it was good. Then God blessed them, saying, "Be fruitful and multiply. Let the fish fill the seas and let the birds multiply on the earth." Genesis 1:20.

Each was producing offspring of the same kind. Likewise, with vegetation, it was "fruitful," because God created seed-bearing plants. "God created human beings in His own image; in the image of God He created them; male and female He created them. Then God blessed them and said, be fruitful and multiply. Fill the earth and govern it." Genesis 1:28.

That is how God created the world and all that is in it; plants, animals, and humans were to reproduce and multiply. Life is a miracle and not to be taken lightly or discarded as rubbish; human life is sacred at any stage of life.

Multiplying by having children is often part of marriage. Children are very precious to God, as is each one of us. "You made all the delicate, inner parts of my body and knit me together in my mother's womb. Thank you for making me so wonderfully complex! Your workmanship is marvelous – how well I know it. You watched me as I was being formed in utter seclusion, as I was woven together in the dark of the womb. You saw me before I was born. Every day of my life was recorded in your book. Every moment was laid out before a single day had passed. How precious are your thoughts about me, O God? They cannot be numbered!" Psalm 139:13.

This scripture shows the heart of God for each human life even before he/she is born. Every baby has a life set before him/her. God has destined it before the baby is even conceived or born. Matthew 10:30 says that He knows how many hairs are on our heads, how precious we are in His sight. If He knows how many hairs are on our heads which seems so insignificant, no thing or unborn baby is too small or unimportant to our God. This can be hard for us to fathom if we never experienced being important to anyone before.

We should be very careful how we raise our children, knowing full well how precious they are to God and protecting them rather than using or abusing them. "And anyone who welcomes a little child like this on my behalf is welcoming me, but if you cause one of these little ones who trusts in me to fall into sin, it would be better for you to have a large millstone tied around your neck and be drowned in the depths of the sea." Matthew 18:5.

"One day some parents brought their children to Jesus so he could lay his hands on them and pray for them. But the disciples scolded the parents for

46

bothering Him. But Jesus said, "Let the children come to me. Don't stop them! For the Kingdom of Heaven belongs to those who are like these children." Matthew 19:13-15.

Jesus showed love, care and respect for children. He wants us to bring our children to Him. He wants us to pray for them and to bless them. We need to pray, bless and speak into our children's lives. It should be a regular part of our everyday lives. Speak the destiny of the Lord into them. This will nurture their spirits and give them vision and hope. Speak hope, life and encouragement to them.

Our children should not be like hired hands or waiting on us hand and foot. Nor should they be like punching bags to let out our frustrations. They are very precious human beings, created by God, who are part of us and our spouses. They are given to us for a short time to love and care for and to teach them about life, God and His ways. We are accountable for how we treat them.

Life is a long journey. When we choose our mates, they must be compatible because they will be with us for life here on earth. They should be our best friends. Many are married for over 30, 40, 50, 60 and some even over 70 years. At the writing of this book I will honor my mother and father who celebrated their 65th wedding anniversary. He passed on to heaven only three months after their anniversary during the writing of this book. Their steadfastness has been a strong example to me. As I was growing up, they showed affection towards each other and took walks holding hands, demonstrating that affection is not outgrown.

After years of marriage, there are still many ups and downs. It is during those times that we learn to get along better and we are bound closer together through the trials. God uses both our good times and hard times to make us better individuals. Marriage takes work to last a lifetime. Let us each remember that our husband or wife is God's special child and very precious to Him and should be to us as well.

I have seen it over and over when a couple goes through a terrible time. When they either break up or almost break up, when they are restored they are stronger than ever. Their love is stronger and renewed as in their youth. God restores all things! The restoration can happen quickly or take time.

Sometimes marriage can be easy and lots of fun, but when we least expect it, it can become difficult and take a lot of work; it can be very stressful, especially when we have stopped nurturing it. At times, It may be so taxing that we may feel there is no way we can get through it. Basically, we have to deal with each other's issues and imperfections, but it helps us to grow.

Each of us has issues to be dealt with. Two different people from two different lives and backgrounds come together and become ONE. We are bound to have differences, discomforts and struggles fitting into each other's wants, needs and expectations. We must give each other the room to grow, to blossom and to spread our wings in order to be all that we can become in God and to continue to grow as a human being.

We each need to be free to creatively express who we are in God. Most of this needs to be done side by side, together. We should be close and supportive of each other, "helping" each other. Not distant and uncaring.

We need to continue to keep in mind the question of, "how will we get through this?" Look to God and He will show you. Do not rely on outside solutions, like emotionally relying on the opposite sex, to help your marriage. This can be a trick of the enemy; look inside the marriage.

Looking for a person outside of the marriage for a solution may be an escape from the marriage and an indication of an unwillingness to work things out. It is a much more painful and sinful way to go. Find a way through, not out! Communicate. Restore the communication. Share your wants and needs. This is basically what a counselor would do for you. You can choose a Christian Counselor if you can't communicate on your own.

Marriage is a gift that God gives us here on earth. It is a mystery. How can we become "one" with another yet be separate individuals? It is a mirror image of how Father God is with Jesus and the Holy Spirit, one yet separate beings. This is also how God sees us with Himself as well. When we are born of the Spirit, we become one with God the Father, Son and Holy Spirit and we live this similar "oneness" with our spouse as well. It is a spiritual phenomenon.

When we take our wedding vows, we are bonded together by those vows and covenant promises. When we have consummated the marriage, it is sealed. We become ONE, making the marital union complete. It is a beautiful thing because God created it! We can see couples being molded together.

When we first get married, there is a time of adjustment. It is very important for newlyweds to take quality time to be together for the emotional union. Some believe that you should not marry at a time when one will be away extensively or working too much. It is good to wait for a time when you can properly take that time to emotionally grow together.

When we are dating or engaged, we think so much about each other and can't wait to see one another. We talk for hours and snuggle and cuddle. When we get married, that should not change. I've heard people say they do not want to marry because the relationship changes after your married. It does not have to change. Often it may, and this can be very painful for those who expect things to be the same as before they took their vows. They may feel unloved, neglected, abandoned, forgotten, and very confused. It makes for a difficult adjustment or transition to married life.

One may feel he/she made a mistake. It is a terrible heartache we do not want to cause the one we marry. Take great care in loving your beloved. Take the time to bond with him/her. We are called to love our spouses unconditionally with a godly love. The enemy prowls and is looking to attack. I have seen people give more attention and affection to their dogs than their spouse and children. This should not be so. Some find it hard to show or feel love. If your parents were not loving to each other it may be difficult to love or show love to your spouse.

Some find it easy to love and be affectionate to babies and young children but find it difficult to love teenagers. This comes from receiving love as a young child but not receiving proper love as a teen; therefore they don't know how to love and accept a teen. Of course those who did not receive proper love and affection as children will not know how to give it to their own children when they come, whether younger or older. Often children have grandparents, foster parents or someone who were role models of giving love. I have seen these people overcome and properly give their children love and affection.

You may realize there are issues of not being able to love your children in the way you began when they were born. It is a fact that teens who plan pregnancies do so for the unconditional love they believe they will receive from their infant. This also can take place in single or married adults when they did not receive the love they needed when they were children. The individual may not even realize it or it may be known and be very disturbing to them. This can cause a couple to want many children to feel the euphoria over, and over again. For some people as the children grow older it is difficult to love them, especially as teens.

If this is you, you are not bad, but what has happened you do not know how to love if you were not loved at those certain childhood stages. This can be very disturbing. You may have made some vows that you would never do this, but now that you are doing the very thing you vowed you wouldn't you may be full of guilt and shame. This is generational and needs prayer and you need to overcome to stop this from passing on to your kids. Your kids need love, and loving, affectionate touch just as you needed it. You can put an end to it.

This also can begin as early as when the infant is in the womb, birth, or infancy when the mother or father does not feel love for the child. This again is because you were not loved at that stage in life. Infants can feel and sense if they are loved or not. God heals! There is hope!

Prayer for Inability to Love your Child or Spouse

First you must acknowledge you judged your parent for not loving you and that you have negative feelings against the parent for this. Repent for this and for not loving them and judging them. Repent for harboring unforgiveness, bitterness, judging and any vows made against them. I will never...kind of vows. I will never be like them. I will never love them. I will never let them be near my kids. I will never forgive them. I hate them. No matter how your parent was to you, right or wrong, you must forgive them and acknowledge your own sinfulness through it. You have not honored them and we get hurt through this.

Next repent for not loving your own children and doing the very thing your parent did to you. Lord, I am so sorry for not loving my children as I should. Lord I forgive my mother/father. Break this process of reaping and sowing off my life, in Jesus' Name. In forgiving we can realize that they, like you had a similar upbringing.

This is a generational issue. It would be beneficial to read over the generational prayers. There may be generational spirits causing an obstacle to block love through unforgiveness, bitterness, abuse, anger, judging, control, manipulation, fear, etc. Repent for sinning in each area that applies.

Look at your parent and make a list of what you see as sins. Next look at yourself and add to the list. You'll see that many will be the same. Often we don't realize it. You can ask spouse, they may see. Now take each issue and pray in faith. Lord, I renounce the generational spirit of unloving in Jesus' Name. I renounce the generational spirits of anger, In Jesus' Name. I renounce the generational spirit of verbal abuse, in Jesus' Name. Etc. I renounce all generational spirits that attack me and my family, in Jesus' Name, amen. Cover us all with your Precious Blood, Jesus. (See 'generational spirits' in generational prayers.)

Last step, ask God to teach you how to love. He loved you before you were even created. While you were being knitted in your mother's womb...He was there loving you. When you were sad and lonely in life...He was there with you through it all. Holding you and loving you. Receive that Love. Get in touch with His Love. His Love is healing. Ask Him to teach you proper affection towards your husband and your children. Ask God to give you His love for them, in Jesus' Name, amen.

Many are married around the age of 21, give or take a few years; there is still a lot of growing and maturing to come since they have just become adults. It is important that we grow and mature together. Both will be immature on certain issues and ten years down the road many weak areas will mature.

Being possessive and controlling comes from our own insecurities. Being possessive, overbearing or abusive to our spouses can stunt them as human beings, like imprisoning them. There is no excuse for abuse; it should never happen. We must remember this is the life God gave them, with us. Their life is very precious, and by honoring them we honor God. We are accountable for how we treat them, for making or breaking their precious gift of life. Their lives are in our hands. Both men and women will flourish in every area they are encouraged. We don't realize how much we tear down with our tongue instead of encouraging one another. Try to be aware of this.

"Treat her as you should so your prayers will not be hindered." 1 Peter 3:7. Did you ever wonder why your life may not be going well with you? Or why your prayers just seem to be blocked? Treating our beloved wrongly hinders us as Christians, and our prayers will not be heard. Your spouse only has one life here on earth, and you need to make the best of it together, treating them as precious as God sees them. Your own life will be blessed by doing so.

This applies to our children as well. They are precious lives in our hands for a short time. How we treat them has a great impact on their formation. The first six years are the foundation to the rest of their lives. [1]When that foundation is cracked it cannot hold up a life properly. The wounds at this time strongly affect the rest of their lives and who they will become, their strengths and their weaknesses. Hopefully, if guarded and shaped properly, they will be strong and emotionally healthy adults. This is why the enemy tries to strike them young; the effects ripple throughout their life and affect not only their future but also future generations to come.

We are accountable for how we take care of them. We need to take this seriously. Too many are abused in many different ways today. These children are entrusted to us to love and care for, not to let out our frustrations on, use for child labor or abuse. They are to be nurtured and loved and cared for.

A word to step parents, the same goes for you, especially with the ones who are totally missing a mother or father, you are it. You are the one standing in that place. When a child lacks love from either the mother or father it has lasting effects on the child. Kick yourself in the bottom and make yourself treat them right with love, and the appropriate affection they need. They need your encouragement. You are accountable before God in how you treat them. Don't be a Cinderella syndrome where your children get favoritism and the others get mistreated or ignored. If they are special enough to get your discipline then they should be special enough to get your love and tenderness. A kind and uplifting word or compliment goes a long ways with a child.

I have ministered to many adults, and I have to say, I am appalled at the severity of the abuse way too many children have had to endure at such a young and innocent age. When they grow into adults, they cannot function properly because they were harmed at the foundation of their lives. This impacts the outcome of their lives. When a young child is not properly taken care of, or loved, he/she seems to spend his/her whole adult life seeking to get that need met, often in all the wrong ways.

Because the first six years are such a vital time in a young child's life, it is very important if at all possible for the mother to be there full time, unless the father is there full time to fill in for the security and proper development of the child.

So many are going to work right after the children are born and handing newborn infants over to people they don't even know. Many are abused and even if they are not abused, nobody can love your child like you. What the child needs is the parent, not a caregiver, but a mother to love, nurture and protect him/her full time.

Parenting is a full-time job. It is important to not strain yourself financially. Try to live within your means to be able to stay home for at least those first five to six years. I also urge you to take a look at society and the lack of morality, and consider home schooling your children. Islam, homosexuality, and sex before marriage are already being taught and even encouraged in many schools. You would not regret home schooling. It is not only good for them but disciplines us as parents. The only regret I have is not doing it sooner. The effects from public school were terrible on my children.

When I look back at my own life, my mother was with me every day during my first five years. I felt such a tangible security in that. What must these kids feel these days when turned over to strangers as newborns so their mothers can go back to work? Then when they get home, they have so much to do to catch up on housework that there is not much left for the kids, let alone their husband. I realize that it often can't be helped. I know that many have to work outside the home, I am sharing the ideal. Be aware though, we must spend extra one-on-one time with those children being raised by others. Question your children and do surprise visits to the caregiver to see how the children are being treated. Many mothers work hours when the fathers can watch the children while they are at work. This is the best alternative. Many have the grandparents which comes in second best but don't forget there is a reason why older people don't have children. Often times they do not have the energy to keep up with your little ones. I have often seen young mothers overuse people and they will often get burned out.

It is hard to juggle spouse and babies. This can be the most rewarding time in our life but very difficult as well. Women struggle to keep their individuality. It seems to get lost in the children and parenting. They can lose sight of not only the husband who needs love and attention, but may lose sight of themselves as well.

After the kids are in bed, there seems to be nothing left to give out, especially when there is more than one young child. It is at this time men can feel to be "second best," ignored or unloved, because now all their beloved's time, attention, and love is being poured out upon of the children. On the other hand, it also is a time when women really need the help of the father to lighten the load. It can be very draining and lonely time during this time in life for the mother. She craves adult conversation and fellowship. Mothers need to be very careful to keep in contact with other mothers and mothering groups, especially when they are not working outside the home, but even when they are working.

Parents consist of two people, mother and father. It is lovely to see a father take plenty of time to love and raise the children with his wife. More fathers are changing the diapers, lending a hand and even helping with the home schooling. In order for children to grow properly, they need good quality time, love and godly affection and cuddling with both mother and father.

Love and affection between the mother and father is also very important for the children to see so they know what a healthy relationship looks like. If mother and/or father do not treat their spouse correctly, the child will learn wrongly. For example, treating your spouse with no respect, treating them like they are your child rather than an adult, verbal, or physical abuse. Often the child will treat his/her spouse in the very same way whether they agree with it or not. It is learned behavior.

If the father figure is not present, there are needs not met within the child. This will have a negative effect on both boys and girls. Unfortunately, many today are raised by a single parent. I have heard adults share on growing up in a single parent home. Some share about being unable to properly fit into the parenting or spousal role. This is because that role was a missing piece of the puzzle of their life. A child should not have to feel they only have one parent when two parents are involved in a family, meaning one or both parents are too busy physically, or emotionally to take part in the lives of their children. Some instances cannot be helped like death or one gone to war, but if at all possible, we need to try hard to be loving parental figures in our children's lives. This can be a trick of the enemy to harm the future of our children.

Be the proper role in your spouse's and children's lives. Read books on parenting to better educate yourself on parenting. Even if you did not have the proper mother or father figure in your life, learn from your parent's mistakes; they don't have to be repeated generation after generation. It can stop with you. Do not fall into the same pitfalls. Spend time with them, read to them, play sports with them, and most important communicate with them. Whether they are two or sixteen, they need you. Make them feel loved, important, and respected. This forms a healthy adult.

"All Scripture is inspired by God and is useful to teach us what is true and to make us realize what is wrong in our lives. It corrects us when we are wrong and teaches us to do what is right. God uses it to prepare and equip His people to do every good work." 2 Timothy 3:16.

This is why I am using so much Scripture in this book. The Scriptures have a lot to say about husbands and wives. I encourage you to read the Bible to better educate yourself on how to live. It is a roadmap to a better life.

"Fathers, do not aggravate your children, or they will become discouraged." NLT Colossians 3:21. The NIV says, don't "embitter" your children.

The Amplified version of Colossians 3:21 says, "Fathers do not provoke or irritate or fret your children – do not be hard on them or harass them; lest they become discouraged and sullen and morose and feel inferior and frustrated; do not break their spirit." We want to create peace and harmony in our homes and in the hearts of our family. We need to nurture their spirits, not break them.

Apparently fathers may have a tendency to do this more than mothers. We must raise our children with love, encouragement and with the fruits of the Spirit. Discipline out of love, not anger or temper; correct and discipline in a way that equally matches the wrong done, is age appropriate, not over-reacting. Raise them with love, patience, kindness, gentleness, compassion, protection, teaching, imparting faith, godliness, purity, and earnestly interceding for them throughout their lives.

We must remember that we must expect our children will make mistakes and do wrong things, as we did as well. Often we act surprised, as if our children should be perfect. Are we perfect? No, they are young and need to be taught and disciplined appropriately. Don't be surprised, expect they need to grow in wisdom and character as Jesus Himself did. Jesus did not sin, our children will. Some worse than others but we must train them up in the way they should go.

"Train a child in the way he should go, and when he is old he will not turn from it." Proverbs 22:6.

"Jesus grew in wisdom and stature and in favor with God and men." Luke 2:52.

Here are some other wise Scriptures that are important to our marriage and family too, because our children learn what they see.

"A quarrelsome wife is as annoying as constant dripping." Proverbs 19:13.

"It is better to live alone in the desert than with a quarrelsome, complaining wife. Proverbs 21:19.

This was mentioned more than once about women being quarrelsome and complaining. We need to guard your selves from this. Because this was written more than once, it is an indication that women may tend to be this way and need to guard themselves from this.

"A gossip betrays a confidence; so avoid a man [or woman] who talks too much." Proverbs 20:19.

We must guard our tongues and refrain from the sinful act of gossip. If we surrender our natural desires to the Lord, He will help to keep us righteous. God rewards the just and the righteous.

"Who can find a virtuous and capable wife? She is more precious than rubies. Her husband can trust her, and she will greatly enrich his life. She brings him good, not harm, all the days of her life." Proverbs 31:10

Verse 27 "She carefully watches everything in her household and suffers nothing from laziness. Her children stand and bless her. Her husband praises her." Verse 30 "Charm is deceptive, and beauty does not last; but a woman who fears the Lord will be greatly praised."

"To husbands and wives: And further, submit to one another out of reverence for Christ. For wives, this means submit to your husbands as to the Lord. For a husband is the head of his wife as Christ is the head of the church. He is the Savior of His body, the church. As the church submits to Christ, so you wives should submit to your husbands in everything."

"For husbands, this means love your wives, just as Christ loved the church. He gave up His life for her to make her holy and clean, washed by the cleansing of God's word. He did this to present her to Himself as a glorious church without a spot or wrinkle or any other blemish. Instead, she will be holy and without fault. In the same way, husbands ought to love their wives as they love their own bodies. For a man who loves his wife actually shows love for himself. No one hates his own body but feeds and cares for it, just as Christ cares for the church. And we are members of His body."

"As the Scriptures say, a man leaves his father and mother and is joined to his wife and the two are united into one. This is a great mystery, but it is an illustration of the way Christ and the church are one. So again I say, each man must love his wife as he loves himself and the wife must respect her husband." Ephesians 5:21-33.

"Both" are to submit to one another. How special that is. Men are to treat their wives, and children, as

Christ did the church. Jesus was many things. He served. He washed their feet, and He laid down his life for love of them. He taught them, healed them and delivered them. He forgave them even when they crucified Him. He prayed for them, "Father forgive them, for they know not what they do". I can't tell you how many through the years we laid hands on each other and our children for healing and deliverance. This is our role.

I remember a time when God was asking me to lay down my life for my daughter and home school her. It was very difficult. She had difficulty learning and teachers at school did not want to deal with her or give her the time and love she deserved and needed.

What a sacrifice this was for me since I had a part-time job and she was already in school. I was a parent who was excited about my little ones starting school so I could dig deeper into God and have more time to myself while getting a part-time job during school hours.

I was looking forward to doing something for me. Home schooling was not part of my agenda. It would take great discipline since she had such difficulty learning. I struggled and struggled with it and said, "Lord, I cannot give her what the other kids in school are getting." His answer was to me was so loud, clear and convicting. "Who said I want those things for her?" "If you cannot lay your life down for your daughter, who can you lay your life down for?" I was so deeply convicted in my heart! Those words supernaturally delivered me from my selfishness.

My daughter deserved my best. My best was to lay my life down for her, and that is what I did. Not of my own to brag, but the Lord gave me the strength to do it. She will be forever blessed by that. When she graduated from home school, she gave a speech that blessed me very much. She spoke of really appreciating the sacrifice I had made and knowing first hand how much better off she was by being home schooled than going to public school.

We will often be called upon to lay our lives down for our wife, husband and children. They are the most important people in our life. We must lay down our lives for each other, and put them first over our own wants and needs. Sometimes it takes some dying to self to be able to do it. God will help us. When we do this, we are being "Jesus" to them. When we can do this for our family, we will be more willing and free to lay our lives down for others when God calls us to do so. It is in seeking His Will that He will reveal it to us. He is not always calling us to take the easy road. It is in the hard ways we learn to lean on Him for support.

In the late 70s or early 80s, we lived in Southern California, having moved there from New York. I have never lived anyplace where I had such peace and contentment. I absolutely loved living there as if I was created to live there. I loved the climate, the spirituality of the area, and I loved our Christian community. We were serving the Lord and seeing abundant fruit. There seemed to be an open heaven over the area, a Bible-belt region. My husband wanted to go back "home" to New York. He wanted to buy the family land, build his own home and work the land. He knew I loved being in California but would from time to time mention how he wanted to go back and build his dream house. I, of course, shared my love for right where I was and said, "Oh no, I love it here." He never forced the issue, because I was so happy where we were at.

One day while in prayer in my back yard, an angel came to me and said, "Go with your husband back to New York." I had to put my dream of being there aside and submit to my husband. He was so thrilled and excited when I told him that God said "go back to New York." He would not have been content until he had lived his dream. Now that he has done all of that, he can move beyond it. But we were able to raise our children in the beauty and seclusion of the countryside. We were also able to pass it down so our grandchildren could be raised there as well.

I feel it is very important to allow our spouses and children to grow into what God has called them to be, not what *we* feel they should be. Love them for who they are, shaping the children as they grow, seeing their strengths and weaknesses. Love them and encourage them to greater heights. Allow God to shape them with His desire, call and destiny for their lives, not putting your dreams onto them, but His will. Give advice when needed or asked for, but do not be overbearing, pushing feelings upon them or criticizing them. We are all guilty of this more or less.

Listen to what you are saying and how you are saying it. You may be surprised by what you hear. Rewording what we say or using a different tone in our voice or attitude can make a huge difference. Love, accept, bless, encourage and build up. Never tear down. Pray and intercede for them. Allow them to be who they are. Not only pray for them, but also pray with them.

"Wives, submit to your husbands, as is fitting for those who belong to the Lord. Husbands, love your wives and never treat them harshly." Colossians 3:18.

"You wives must accept the authority of your husbands. Then, even if some refuse to obey the Good News, your godly lives will speak to them without any words. They will be won over by observing your pure and reverent lives." Don't be concerned about the outward beauty of fancy hairstyles, expensive jewelry, or beautiful clothes. You should clothe yourselves instead with the beauty that comes from within, the unfading beauty of a gentle and quiet spirit, which is so precious to God. This is how the holy women of old made themselves beautiful. They trusted God and accepted the authority of their husbands." 1 Peter 3:1.

"In the same way, you husbands must give honor to your wives. Treat your wife with understanding as you live together. She may be weaker than you are, but she is your equal partner in God's gift of new life. Treat her as you should so your prayers will not be hindered." 1 Peter 3:7.

"Drink water from your own well — share your love only with your wife." "Let your wife be a fountain of blessing for you. Rejoice in the wife of your youth. She is a loving deer, a graceful doe. Let her breasts satisfy you always, may you always be captivated by her love." Proverb 5:15, 18.

"A worthy wife is a crown for her husband, but a disgraceful woman is like cancer to his bones." Proverbs 12:4.

"The man who finds a wife finds a treasure, and he receives favor from the Lord." Proverbs 18:22.

"So the Lord God caused the man to fall into a deep sleep. While the man slept, the Lord God took out one of the man's ribs and closed up the opening. Then the Lord God made a woman from the rib, and he brought her to the man." Genesis 2:21.

What is a rib? It supports the body, and it protects the heart and vital organs. God created man to support and protect woman. Some early Scriptures say, "God took a part of the man's side." Why the side? The rib is from the side. Not above to lord over, not below to be stepped upon or trampled upon but beside to love each other, to share with each other, to help each other equally and to walk side by side, hand in hand, to be a helper, a companion, and a friend.

Individual or Group Questions

1. What ways can I love more in my marriage?

2. What things do you do for your spouse that shows *your* love for your spouse?

3. In what areas do I need to work on in myself?

4. What problem do you see in your marriage right now? Discuss and find the solution for this problem together to resolve it. Share and "hear" each other's feelings on this issue. Pray for God's heart on this issue...what does "He" say about it? Both seek God in prayer and write His heart on this issue on your life.

5. In What ways can I be a better parent? Step parent?

3

Love

What is Love? Love can be different things to different people depending on their experiences. Some may never have had a hug or received love in their lives; some received very little affection, even from infancy. A person like this would have no idea how to express something he or she never received. They cannot give hugs if they have never received hugs. Maybe they were always let down and hurt all the time. For many, love was very conditional; meaning, if you don't do something for it, you do not receive it, and so you feel you have to work for it. For some, the parents only showed love when the child was being good, so the child thought he/she would only be loved by being good. Some children may misunderstand discipline and correction as hate.

Maybe we felt we had to do things to make our parents notice us or love us, and we felt we had to work for love, attention, or compliments. Maybe another was over-loved and smothered, or another manipulated and controlled. Each of us perceives things differently. Maybe one is married to another who is the opposite, which can cause the person to feel off-balance or left feeling empty and wanting all the time.

Each family experiences love in a certain way; it affects each individual differently. Even two brothers or two sisters in the same family can react differently to the identical way that they were loved or treated. They can perceive situations differently which causes each to judge the situation differently, thus reacting differently. There are many ways of expressing love, and many of us have experienced an incorrect way of love since none is perfect like God. His love is the only perfect, pure love.

Everyone has a way of identifying love. It is good to get to know your spouse's expectation of love. It is his/her love language. There are online tests that both can take. Try to Google, "Love Language Test." This test will show you how you and your spouse expect love. It is good to know this before marriage. One may need to be given gifts, another hugs and affection. Another may be affirmed by telling him or her, "I love you," "You're beautiful." Yet another may need quality time with his or her spouse, or a combination of ways of showing love. For some, working hard to provide for the family may be their way of showing love.

Most often you and your beloved are total opposites. You love others the way you expect to be loved in return. The way you need to be loved may not be understood by your spouse, and his or her way of needing to be loved may not be understood by you. This may leave each of you feeling empty. Once you find out how your spouse expects to be loved, learn all that you can to understand him/her and use it to bless your spouse. Learn to love them the way that fulfills them the most. If it is foreign to you, it may be work and it will probably stretch you. By unselfishly looking to the needs and pouring into the other, you receive so much more in return and no one feels empty or lost. You will feel more fulfilled and loved than you could ever imagine.

Think of this; when you get a new dog or pet, you buy a book and learn all you can about all the details of that particular pet. Many don't do as much for marriage or children.

"Love is patient, love is kind. It does not envy, it does not boast, it is not proud. It is not rude, it is not self-seeking, it is not easily angered, it keeps no record of wrongs. Love does not delight in evil but rejoices with the truth. It always protects, always trusts, always hopes, always perseveres. Love never fails." NIV 1 Corinthians 13:4.

We have all heard this and it is the number one Scripture used in marriage ceremonies. This is how we should be with our spouse, children, and everyone. I like to share God's Love this way. Since God "IS" Love, then I can put His Name in place of Love like this. God is patient, God is kind. He does not envy and He does not boast and is not proud. He is not rude and He is not self-seeking. God is not easily angered and He keeps no record of wrongs. God does not delight in evil but He rejoices with the truth. God never fails. To me, that is Powerful! God is Love itself. Love flows from Him; it is what He is made of. It is His thoughts toward you.

I would like to share a Scriptural experience that I had a number of years ago. The Bible says that a man may have visions and revelations of the Lord, and goes on to tell the story of a man who was caught up into paradise but did not know whether it was in the spirit or his body. (2 Corinthians 12:1-4) Ezekiel and Daniel had similar experiences in the Old Testament as well.

In my vision or experience during prayer, the Holy Spirit took me in spirit to God's throne room. I could see behind me as if through the back of my head. The Holy Spirit was like immense light and fire.

I saw Jesus with a white gown and red sash. I met God our Father; He was sitting on the throne. I also saw Jesus sitting at his right but forward. I had to go through Jesus to get to the Father. When I approached Him, there was absolutely no condemnation. I was so amazed at this. Just pure Love, the purest, strongest Love I have ever experienced. In fact, His whole being was Love and it overflowed from Him and was all around Him. I realized He was LOVE. That is what He is. All pure Love comes from Him and came about from Him. He is the beginning of Love. We learn God is love as little children, and we understand it as adults as God reveals Himself to us, but I learned a very deep firsthand, heavenly revelation of it that day.

Without realizing it, we often see God like our earthly fathers. If our earthly father was condemning and punished harshly, we see God that way too, subconsciously. We cannot see God properly if our father on earth did not treat us properly. No earthly father is perfect, so we look through eyes and heart that are dirty with residue from our hurts of this life and the lives of our ancestors. It is hard to see God for who He really is. It is hard to see anything correctly because our perspective can be warped in lesser or greater degrees.

For some reason, I must have felt God would condemn me because I was surprised about the greatness of His Love and that there was no condemnation. That was my greatest first impression. Something seemed to be screaming, "NO

CONDEMNATION." He was so happy to see me, and I knew they had waited for that moment. Jesus was happy, too, but He seemed to be saving the moment for my Father and me. I was surprised about the greatness of His Love for me. I never *really knew* how wonderful He was even though I had experienced Him in the past here on earth and was born again and spirit-filled, but when I looked at Him all I saw Love. Love flowed from Him and permeated the atmosphere around Him. I realized He not only permeated Love, He *was* Love itself. He was the author of all pure Love. I realized that all Love has come from Him and Him alone.

At another point of this experience, I was in a circle with the Father, the Son and the Holy Spirit. I actually witnessed and experienced the "Oneness" of the Holy Trinity. They were all separate entities, yet One. I was in that circle too, connected. It was like we were holding hands. I was *One* with them as well. It made Jesus' prayer so real to me. "I have given them the glory that you gave me, that they may be One as we are One: I in them and you in me. May they be brought to complete unity to let the world know that you sent me and have loved them even as you have loved me." NIV John 17:22, This was one of His final prayers before laying His life down for us. Jesus laid His life down so that we may become One with God the Father, Son and Holy Spirit. He died so that we would be in complete unity with Them. We are meant to be included! Jesus' prayer confirms this. We are part of the Trinity and working for the Father as well, bringing the Kingdom of God on earth through our lives while being ONE with them. This is here on earth, not when we die and leave this earth. This will show the world He is real and wonderful. This will show our families He is real and awesome!

Our love is not this perfect and neither was our parent's love for us; some were closer to it than others. We learn from our mistakes and theirs. We strive toward being closer to our Lord, to become ONE with the true Love of all, the Triune God. Only then can we become more perfect husbands, wives, mothers and fathers.

We will stumble from time to time with each other's expectations. Dr. John Gray[5] describes men as being from Mars and women from Venus, meaning, just by being male and female, we do things very differently as if we come from different planets. We also filter things differently within ourselves or perceive things differently because of our different upbringing, and our past wounds. Something may bother one person but not the other. Sound like a no win situation? It does not have to be. When we keep God in the center of our marriage, He teaches us and gives us grace and protects our marriage. Things will not always be perfect, and God does let us learn lessons so we grow and mature.

Here is an example of Mars & Venus and one way I identified with Love early in our marriage. When I was growing up, on Christmas and birthdays in our family we received gifts from those who were very close to us and loved us. I unknowingly expected that when someone loves you and that person gives you a gift on these occasions; it's all that I knew. Keep in mind, I had no idea this was an expectation I had. When I turned seventeen for some reason I perceived that my parents gave me a very insignificant, inexpensive gift for my birthday. I was crushed and felt very unloved. I literally saw it as a sign they did not love me. What accompanied this was that they also just dropped the gift in my hands in passing, carelessly; I was crushed. As kids, we can perceive things wrongly or do not get the full picture. Most likely I judged them for this, and later in life I had to repent for that and forgive them. Before long, I grew up and got married.

My husband grew up in a very large family. Perhaps they may not have given gifts as much, because I rarely got them except for Christmas. It was very hard because not realizing it, I identified that with love. When I did not get a gift, I was crushed like a little girl. I was used to having attention on my birthday, being made to feel special and having loved ones celebrate me.

During the first couple of years of marriage, I got birthday gifts, beautiful Valentine's Day gifts and even notes around the house where to look for the gifts. After a couple of years of being married, my husband would go outside, work in the garden or go off doing his own thing when it was my birthday. He literally acted like he forgot my birthday, having no idea I was waiting, wondering and feeling sadly ignored. Year after year I wondered, "Why is he ignoring me?" I didn't know if he forgot my birthday or not. This was unheard of in my world. "Why is he not paying attention to me?" "Why did I not get a gift?"" He must not love me or care about me." My heart was crushed. My children grew up never giving me gifts, because they were not taught by my husband, who just did not do that sort of thing.

Years later, I stopped buying him gifts; what was the point? I thought, "I never get them in return." In my heart, it was done as an act of resentment which was not right. Again, I did not understand that the gift was a form of love that I expected from my husband or children. Your expectations may not always equal your spouse's, especially in the beginning when you are still learning about one another. Basically, we are still learning about ourselves. My husband had no idea I

73

was going through so much anguish because of it. I did not understand my own hurt and expectations enough to explain them to him. I did not think I needed to explain.

I cannot believe how many women have gone through this same experience. I would help friends through the same thing when they were hurt and depressed, because their husbands acted like they forgot their birthday, leaving them feeling sad and depressed.

Your feelings and emotions go through an unbelievable roller coaster as you grow and adjust to one another. One can be bent out of shape from something, and the other has no clue of the heartbreak the other is experiencing over something so simple. This is why communication is so very important and can even spare a lot of unnecessary pain.

From the start, being open and honest about our feelings can resolve many issues as they arise. Of course this goes for many things, not just love. We all have our belief systems. It also pertains to our faith, religious differences, cultural differences, race, or childhood family traditions which may be very different from one another's. It is best to share these before we marry and not hide our true feelings. The better we get to know each other before we marry the smoother the transition.

Both partners may be spiritual, but both could have different beliefs. One may be spirit filled and the other one not. One may believe in signs, wonders and miracles, and the other may not have the faith for those things. There can be a conflict in beliefs in many areas concerning God. Sometimes we put God in our little box and expect Him to only fit into our way of thinking.

We need to stretch to see new facets of God to grow deeper in our faith and deeper in our intimacy with God. Sometimes we get stuck in mindsets that we cannot get ourselves out of, right or wrong. Our mindsets can keep us from growing deeper in God. Just because we think God would never do something, doesn't mean He would not. Just because we think He is a certain way, does not mean He is. God is so far above what we ever expect or dream of.

Each has different expectations, and when they are not fulfilled there is trouble. Often people marry assuming their new husband or wife will fulfill their every hope, dream and expectation. While our husband or wife should fulfill something in us, God is ultimately our complete fulfillment. We both were created for Him, for His pleasure and His fellowship. Only God is our complete fulfillment. When we seek fulfillment in other ways, our lives feel unfulfilled. If we are married and it is not fulfilling us, we must seek God more whole heartedly.

On the other hand, we cannot just ignore our spouse and figure God will take care of them; we have an important role in their lives and that also needs to be fulfilled. God gave us to each other to take care of.

After many years of marriage, I don't expect gifts and now I get them more often. He tries to do better, and it doesn't bother me if I don't get anything. Actually, I expect to get nothing so when I do get something, it is special to me. I prayed and forgave my parents and repented for judging them, and it just doesn't bother me anymore to not get a gift. He has grown, too, and now gives gifts and gives of himself. We both grow in wisdom and understanding as we grow older and come to understand each other better.

We can have expectations of what marriage will be like, consciously or subconsciously. When that does not happen, it can be a very painful experience. I believe many women cannot wait to be with that special one they love for the rest of their lives. Looking forward to not being separated, being together all of the time. Men, on the other hand, often feel once they have their women, it is time to move on with life and be the provider. They do not realize the woman is left wanting because the husband is gone all the time. I find this with many young couples.

Let me explain; I was one of them. When I got married, I assumed I would be with my man. We did not live together before hand, so I could not wait to be with my husband all of the time. Suddenly, all of these jobs came up, one after another and he seemed to be gone all of the time. He was a very good provider, but I wanted my husband. I was very lonely. Just when I thought the jobs were over, he would pick up a few more to take the place of the last job. His way of showing love was working hard and being a good provider. He would also go fishing with co-workers for hours, and I'd be left alone again and again. He'd be working on a car for long hours...it just seemed I was always being left out and always left waiting and wanting. There always seemed to be something to keep us apart. I should have realized the hint when we dated and I would sit for long stretches next to the car he was working under. Love is patient!

The important thing is to not nag. Often one can nag and complain about not being together. So every time you are together you are fighting about how you are never together. Or arguing about how unhappy you are and pushing the spouse away, not making the best of the time you do have together. Men, be aware though that you can close this gap and spend more quality time with your wife. Remember before marriage how you could not wait to be with her? This also means that once kids come, being gone too much not only makes you a part-time husband but a part-time father also. Not only will your wife suffer but the kids will grow up remembering how dad was gone all the time. This also leaves their mom with the needless weight of being a single parent. Often it cannot be helped, but I am talking about what can be helped. I am saying men, but this also may be an issue a woman can have but I have seen it be more common with men.

Our society caters to long hours of work away from our family. We set ourselves up thinking we need all the latest technology which is costly. It is too easy to get into the trap of having to work a lot to pay our debts. I urge you if you haven't already done so, don't use credit! Get into the habit of saving your money first to pay for items rather than pay after. Use your debit card, using money you already have saved. We often work to keep up with the neighbors or to get the newest and best of material items. Really what your family needs is you. Nothing can take the place of you.

Most parents or parents-to-be are so excited for that baby to be born and then in six short weeks they turn their new baby over to strangers and back to work. A mother and father's love and presence is nurturing. Nothing can take the place of the mother and father. We often set ourselves up to the standards of others. We think we need this or that to fulfill us. We came into the world with nothing and we will go out of the world with nothing but our family is everlasting.

Our true fulfillment is not material items but God alone can fill that empty need in our heart. God alone is our fulfillment. I heard it said, "I believe in God and I believe in Christianity but there is more out there." Let me tell you, there is more in Christianity that will never bore you. All the wonderful godly adventures in the Bible are for you too. There are wonderful gifts of God. Christianity is not meant to be boring at all. No life in the Bible was boring or empty. If you are feeling empty don't latch onto material items for fulfillment but God alone can fulfill. There is so much more in God than you will ever know. He created us to have fellowship with Him. The emptiness in your heart was meant for your creator to fill it. People try to fill inner emptiness or inner pain by self medicating themselves with drugs, alcohol, buying things, perversion, sex, money, adultery, and more. Some even have children or marry for this reason and when the husband or wife cannot fulfill them they search on. Seek God and His kingdom first and all else will fall into place. You can never know Him enough. A deeper relationship with God is a life long challenge that you will never regret. I am not talking about religion. Religion can leave you dry and empty. A relationship with the living God is wonderful and a life long process.

Workaholic or Alcoholic

Sometimes when a child is growing up, he or she had to win the approval of a parent by doing good works; they continue to do this as adults when married. This can be the cause of what I always called a workaholic. Unfortunately it greatly clashes when the wife or husband does not need that kind of action to fulfill his or her type of love expectation. It can actually be the opposite for the spouse's needs, especially if the expectation of love is needing and expecting to spend time with the other spouse. If one is very secure, he or she can easily learn to deal or adapt with it and fill the time with pressing hard after God, parenting, work, ministry and other interests and hobbies. This is a perfect time to pursue God deeply; He will use your experiences to draw you closer to Himself.

If someone is an insecure person, it will take much longer to adjust and deal with learning how to cope in marriage when the marriage partner is rarely around. This person may seek to fulfill that need in all the wrong places. If you know God, then you can press into Him and He will help you through. Sometimes, it can push the wife into working hard to please the husband, doing the very thing that was done to her. It is often the men who can become workaholics, but women fall into this as well. She does not realize this, and works hard to keep him home more and is left feeling unfulfilled as a woman or wife. She can grow cold and hard in order to protect her hurting heart. Also, resentment and bitterness can set in if she does not take this to Jesus.

In my life, when my children were born I was left quite often to raise them alone. Now, years later and in hind sight, my husband fully regrets being so absorbed in work and missing so much. When people work so much, it is hard for them to tear away from it, even when they know they need to rest. They feel they have reason to work so hard, and it is a force that keeps them going and they cannot stop. It can be a vicious cycle which leads to a repeated time of feeling overworked and depressed. My husband realized life is not about working all the time, and if he had to do it over again, he would do it differently. Old habits are hard to change.

If this sounds like you or your spouse, know it is not totally your fault. It takes some inner healing to get out of this. First, there is a need to forgive the parents for not having time for the child and forgiving them for not affirming the child enough. We need to forgive the father or mother for working a lot and in many cases not giving enough affection. It also involves repenting for judging the parent for these very things. By judging them for these things, you will do the very thing you hated that they did to you. I find this happens more often in larger families where the parents have so many children and responsibilities that they cannot give each child the individual attention and/or affection he or she needs. Often younger children are demanding of the parent's attention. Because of this older children get ignored or overworked by picking up a lot of the parent's tasks.

Often a child works hard to get the positive affirmation. This vicious cycle can begin in early childhood. After we pray for the things I've mentioned, we need to break the cycle and cover it with the precious blood of Jesus. Put what Jesus did on the Cross and Blood of Jesus between us and this vicious cycle once and for all. Pray also that new habits would be formed and everyone would be fulfilled by healthy roles, in Jesus Name.

There are varying coping mechanisms people use to get through things as they grow up as I mentioned. Alcohol, drugs, shopping, habitual eating, and working are examples of ways people grasp to cope.

I say all this to share the pain I felt early in my marriage when it took a turn in a direction that I did not expect. It was very painful, especially in the early years. I share this to say that you must be mindful if you are neglecting your spouse; be aware if your spouse's needs are not being met. How does God view being apart a lot when newlyweds? Deuteronomy 24:5 says, "A newly married man must not be drafted into the army or be given any other official responsibilities.

He must be free to spend one year at home, bringing happiness to the wife he has married."

Many are oblivious and do not even notice or care if their spouse is happy or if their needs are taken care of. Care and listen! If you want your marriage to last, you must care. Make your marriage priority. God obviously set the marriage apart for the first year for that bonding to set in. It is these kinds of things that harm a marriage and push people to seek attention and affection in wrong places. It is the very thing that causes people to be unhappy in their marriages and want out because they feel unloved and uncared for. What does God say about that? "He must not deprive her of food, clothing and marital rights. If he does not provide her with these three things, she is to go free, without any payment of money." NIV Exodus 21:10:11. The NLT says "If he fails in any of these three obligations, she may leave as a free woman." What are marital rights? Is it sexual intimacy? But how about love, nurturing, cherishing, being kind to, and not being abusive in any way? Remember your vows; have you broken them? If you do not love, then you have broken your vows. God said she is free to go by grounds of neglect. Let us not neglect our spouse in any way.

Being left alone all the time can cause one to feel neglected. There is no marriage if it feels like the husband or wife has dropped out of the picture, especially if it happens right from the start. There is no time for roots to take hold and bonding to take place. This is one of the reasons, I believe, God felt it was so important for newlyweds to spend extra time together. When one is not being fulfilled from the start, It can also push one consciously or subconsciously to look for happiness elsewhere for example in other people of the opposite sex. Again, I know with jobs it is not always possible and seasoned and godly marriages can often handle being apart, others cannot.

Create things for you and your spouse to do. Try scheduling time to be together if you have to, and discipline yourself to stop looking for work to do and make your husband or wife important. It will be noticed. Now I have to tell you. It came to the point that my husband did not have to look for work, it found him. So learning to say no is important too. It will make a difference in your marriage. Maybe it can't be helped; you may have to make the time very special that you have together.

Sweep them off their feet. Keep your love alive by nurturing it. A fire goes out unless you keep putting logs on it. Let your spouse know that he or she is special just like you did before you were married. If you cannot be together very much, I will repeat, make the time you have together very special. You cannot expect a marriage to be healthy or be good if it is ignored. It takes work and tender loving care; your spouse is worth it. Your marriage is worth it.

The expectations we have can come in a variety of ways. Because your mother or father did things one way, maybe you expect your spouse to follow suit. Your spouse's parents may have done things totally different, so his expectations will be different. No two parents are alike; not wrong, just different.

Here is another example of a young newlywed couple. She grew up with a lot of love and wholesome hugs and kisses. He grew up with no love and absolutely no touching unless it was hitting and abuse. When they married, she needed affection to which she was accustomed. He gave her a lot of affection before marriage. As soon as they married, he worked a lot and when he came home he wanted to be alone. She had been alone all day and couldn't wait for him to come home. She vocalized that she needed more hugs, kisses, and attention. He called her spoiled by her parents because they gave her so much love. Care, care about what your spouse shares with you. Stretch yourselves to meet in the middle.

We really don't even know we are expecting things; we just automatically do, and unconsciously expect them to be just like us. This is a perfect time to start your own traditions for your family. You do not need to be a carbon copy of your parents or your in-laws. Remember, it is a mix of both of your ways that makes your family special; it can't *always* be one of you that gets his/her own way all of the time to dictate and control. It would not be fair. One is not always right, that would be out of balance. Our spouse will challenge us and stretch us. We will definitely grow as a person.

When we are unhappy in or with our marriage, we must share it with our spouse before anger or bitterness settles in our heart. Share it humbly and lovingly, peacefully and honestly from your heart. Trust me; it will be received much better that way. It is hard to hear we are doing something wrong; it can be very painful. It is much easier to hear when shared in love. It is very easy to take offense, but it is best to listen humbly and care. Take time and let God work with you. God does speak to us through our spouse. You must care and take to heart what your spouse is sharing. We no longer are living alone; we are two in the marriage, and we must take an attitude of caring about what the other is saying. We must take it to God and try to understand the other. God will help us. When it comes right down to it, I am sure you would not want your beloved wife or husband to be unhappy in your marriage. Marriage is no place for self-centeredness or wanting to be left alone. You are no longer one, but of course we all need some alone time.

Once we marry and begin parenting, we begin reaping the judgments we made against our parents when they were married and parenting. Somehow this does not start to happen until we are at that same stage in life. This is why we do not see these things before marriage. It kicks in right afterwards. We reap what we have sown. Honoring our mother and father is SO important, because where we dishonor and where we judge, is the very area in which we begin to reap[3]. All of a sudden, we actually become the parent we said we would never be and do the very things we vowed we would never do. We do not even know we are going to be like this until we reach that stage. We may not even realize we are being just like the negative in our parents. Trust me, your spouse can see it; they know.

When a marriage is in trouble, it is not the marriage itself that is in trouble. It is personal healing that is needed for the individuals and dealing with personal past hurts and the dishonoring, the judgments and the generational curses which passed through the generational line to us. It is best, if possible, to work on this before you even marry and before your children are conceived. It takes simple spoken prayers of faith through the authority God has given us in Jesus' Name. Otherwise, you will be living the sins of your father, mother, and your ancestors. None of our parents were perfect. They all sinned, and we all sin. It needs to be dealt with. We have sinned by our own decisions and actions, and we suffer the consequences for what we've done not only now but especially in the past when we were young children.

We can go through simple prayers and it is best that you do it with your spouse or fiancé'. Let's face it, a marriage that prays together stays together. Start off right with the habit of regular prayer and reading of the Word together; it's never too late to begin. It is not easy; our flesh will rebel, but start the habit to regularly pray and read the Bible together.   If not together, you should be doing reading your Bible regularly by yourself. You both need to go through these prayers. No one is exempt. If you go through these prayers, you will be more healed by the end of this book. If you don't think you need it, do it by faith anyway; it cannot hurt.

I want to take a moment to address alcoholism and the other issues listed. If you can identify with your issue, you can follow it to the root of how it got there. Most likely something was not fulfilled by the parent(s) or you were hurt deeply by someone. Follow to what that is. You address it just like the workaholic or alcoholic; you must admit you have a problem. Most people say, "I can stop whenever I want. I just don't want to." Or they can stop for a short while to prove to themselves and others that they can stop, and then they go right back to it. Admit you have a problem.

Forgive your parents or the person for what you feel they did when you were a child. Are you willing to forgive them? Again, this does not make what they did right or wrong. It releases you from the incident. Maybe they were not there for you, or one of them is an alcoholic. Maybe they appeared to love a sibling more. Maybe you didn't feel loved by them. Our perception is not always correct as children, and sometimes we read it exactly right. Either way we must forgive. Forgive from your heart. You may need to do this more than once or twice. We keep forgiving until it goes from our head to our heart. Follow the example I spoke of. Except if we are an alcoholic, chances are a parent was as well and/or our ancestors.   Use the prayer for generational curses.

Prayers for Generational Curses

A. Repent for the sins of the fathers.

First we repent for their sins which caused the curse to start flowing down through the generations. You can just say: **I repent for the sins, judgments, rejection, and disobedience against you Lord, of my mother and father, and grandparents, maternal and paternal, and great grandparents on my mother's side and my father's side and their mothers and fathers in Jesus' Name. (Name the sins, if known) I repent for the sin of____.**

I am going to explain after each step to help you understand. Next time you use the prayers you can skip the explanation. We stand in for our ancestors and repent for their sins whether they are dead or living. (That is our mother/father/their mother and father, and their mother and father on maternal and paternal sides where the sin began and the generations through which the sin has filtered down in the DNA, at least four generations.) Look at this as similar to when a doctor asks if a disease runs in your family. That, too, is generational and the medical field knows about it; it is the very same with sin and curses. You can pray in the same way against sicknesses or curses as well. These need to be cut out of our generational line and separated from us by the work Jesus did on the cross, covered by the Blood of Christ.

"I lay the sins of the parents upon their children; the entire family is affected, even children in the third and fourth generations of those who reject me, but I lavish unfailing love for a thousand generations on those who love me and obey my commands." NLT Exodus 20:5. "Yet He does not leave the guilty unpunished; he punishes the children and their children for the sin of the fathers to the third and fourth generation." NIV Exodus 34:7.

We need to pray to break that. Now you may say, "The Blood of Christ cancels that out." If so, then why are there so many sick born-again Christians? Why are so many dying of the same diseases that their parents or relatives had? Why is alcoholism in a family carried down? Why aren't Christians whole and overcoming? We must break the curse, and we can "because" of the cross.

"For God in all His fullness was pleased to live in Christ, and through Him God reconciled everything to Himself. He made peace with everything in heaven and on earth by means of Christ's Blood on the cross." Colossians 1:19-20.

"You were dead because of your sins and because your sinful nature was not yet cut away. Then God made you alive with Christ, for He forgave all our sins. He canceled the record of the charges against us and took it away by nailing it to the cross. In this way, He disarmed and stripped away all authority and power of the spiritual rulers and authorities. He shamed them publicly by His victory over them on the cross." Colossians 2:13.   Spiritual rulers and authorities do still try to take authority and can, if we allow them to.

Take these scriptures and make them your personal prayer. That is praying the scriptures. I encourage you to practice praying the scriptures. Let's practice with Colossians 2:13. **I was dead because of my sins, because my sinful nature was not yet cut away. God, you make me alive with Christ. You forgive all my sins. You canceled the record of charges against me and took it away by nailing my**

sin to the cross. Disarm and strip away all authority and power of the spiritual rulers and authorities. I have victory through Jesus' victory over them on the cross. In Jesus Name, Amen.

I feel this is why we need to place the cross between us and the sin, or curse, and the process of reaping what we sowed, because His blood on that cross stops it from coming upon us and our future generations. Satan is a liar and will try to get away with attacking us even though he knows we have the victory. If we are fooled that he has power and we have none, we let the enemy have his way; he wins. He only has the power that we allow him to have. So take authority now through Jesus' blood, shed on the cross. God does allow satan to attack us for our own growth. It makes us stronger when we fight against him. It also teaches us so we can help others.

"Continue to work out your salvation in fear and trembling." Philippians 2:12. Since we are working out our salvation, it is not complete. We are not perfect. Salvation in the Greek is called *sozo*. Sozo means the complete, wholeness of our salvation; Saved, Healed and Delivered!

For some reason, many get a hold of their salvation and believe in their salvation but they do not get a hold of their healing or deliverance. They have trouble believing for their healing. They are still walking around sick. The proof is in the fact that so many in the Body of Christ are still sick and dying of diseases. The enemy is getting away with too much. We are letting him, and it is time we took our authority and stopped him once and for all. The enemy makes us feel helpless, but we are not helpless, we are Sons of God. The enemy puts that helpless feeling upon us. Shake it off! If Jesus is the King of kings, we are the King's kids.

Know you have authority because of who your Father is. You are royalty!

Look for repetitive issues. The only reason the curse carries through is because everyone who is tempted falls into sin. Be the first to overcome; that curse will shrivel up and die. "Resist the devil and he will flee." Break his assignment off from you. **I repeat A again:**

A. Repent for the sins of the fathers.
I repent for the sins, judgments, rejection, and disobedience against you Lord, of my mother and father, and grandparents, maternal and paternal, and great grandparents on my mother's side and my father's side and their mothers and fathers in Jesus' Name. (Name the sins, if known) I repent for the sin of_____.

Next is forgiving judgments made against others, specifically against our parents. A judgment is defined and taught by John Sandford in his Basic 1 teaching, chapter 3. He says that "there is depth and power of bitter root judgments which have a life of their own. They are one of the most potent forces behind the recurring patterns of trouble and/or destruction in our lives. The power of bitter roots comes from the unchangeable laws of God, which cause us to reap in kind what we have sown."

B. Forgive them of their sins and judgments. Name the specific sins, if you know them. Father forgive them for their sin of_____. Examples: alcoholism, addictions, drug abuse, adultery, divorce, children out of wedlock, anger, rape, witchcraft, occult practices, etc... You can look at your family and see what has been repeating itself generation after generation. Some are obvious because you see them or the repeated effects of them on your family members such as brothers and sisters, aunts, uncles, parents and grandparents. Or you may have heard stories carried down through the generations. What negative emotions do you carry? What negative issues keep arising like poverty, financial problems, bad things happening to you regularly, sicknesses, diseases, etc? You may think what good is this, my ancestors are dead; but there are no limitations of time or space with God. Prayer changes things in the spiritual realm for you and me in the now. It can literally change the reaping and sowing process that is still alive and active. Ask the Lord to reveal to you and in your life; as he reveals, you can break the judgments and walk in God's healing power.

"I tell you the truth, whatever you bind on earth will be bound in heaven and whatever you loose on earth will be loosed in heaven. Again, I tell you that if two of you on earth agree about anything you ask for, it will be done for you by my Father in heaven. For where two or three come together in my name, there am I with them." NIV Matthew 18:18-20. You can do these prayers alone, by yourself, but it is more effective doing it with at least one other person to agree with you in prayer.

C. Plead the Blood of Jesus through the generational line. There is power in the Blood! Break off the effect of curse from the sin, where it began, down to you, to the end of time…off of you and your offspring, to the end of time, which you and your children and future generations will be blessed and not cursed, in Jesus' Name. Ask the Father to change the very DNA that was affected by this curse. Remove the curse from your DNA and your children's DNA, in Jesus' Mighty Name.

D. Place the cross between you and the sin, the curse, and the process of reaping what you or others have sown.

E. Confess and Repent for your own sins and have the person praying with you forgive you your sin, in Jesus' Name. Do this audibly. If alone say, "I accept God's forgiveness in the Name of Jesus.

"If we confess our sins, He is faithful and righteous to forgive us our sins and to cleanse us from all unrighteousness." 1 John 1:9.

"Confess your sins to each other and pray for each other so that you may be healed. The earnest prayer of a righteous person has great power and produces wonderful results." James 5:16.

By confessing our sins, we obtain forgiveness and healing, and that is what we are going for... wholeness. It is important to live a righteous life so that our prayers have power. It is important to walk in power and not be lukewarm so that we can be used more for the Kingdom of God. Jesus walked in authority and power and we should also.

2 Tim 3:5 warns, "They will act religious, but they will reject the power that could make them godly. Stay away from people like that." We can only become godly by the power of God; nothing of our self can do this. We want to be more like Jesus and Jesus walked in power and authority. Many churches reject the power of the Holy Spirit that is taught in the Bible.

F. Break the generational curse in Jesus' Name. Put the cross of Christ between you and the curse, also between you and the judgments that were

sown. Include your spouse, your children and your grandchildren to the end of time.

As you look at your family what sins come to mind? List and pray: I renounce all sins of my ancestors and family. I renounce the generational spirit of _____. (Example-I renounce the spirit of generational lust. I renounce the generational spirit of fear) I cut all ties and bonds they have had on me. Tie any lose ends with you Lord Jesus. Thank you Lord, In Jesus' Name I pray. Amen.

Paul Cox shares an example of this in his book, Discernment Training and Generational Deliverance. "A lady recently shared an experience she had as she began to renounce a spirit of generational anger. Pressure on her throat due to a demonic presence made it very difficult to speak the words. She recognized and acknowledged this strong demonic hold on her family line and renounced it. As a strong Christian, she was shocked that she could be oppressed by a demon passed down through the generations."

Be sure to pray to release all the blessings due to you from your family line. Call down in Jesus Name, all gifts, and blessings left dormant and unclaimed to you and your family. Return seven times what the enemy has stolen. May all the blessings continue for a thousand generations. Call them down upon you and your family, in Jesus' Name. Ask the Lord to teach you new righteous ways and to renew your mind. Ask Him to cleanse every dark area of your soul, In Jesus' Name, Amen.

Say these prayers and more as the Holy Spirit leads you together or with someone who will agree with you in prayer, preferably your fiancé, husband, wife, or a strong Christian who knows who they are in Christ. Now that you have these prayers you can do this whenever God reveals things to you.

Individual or Group Questions

1. What is my identification of love? In what ways do I most feel loved by my spouse/fiancé?

2. In what ways can my spouse or fiancé show love better?

3. Finish this question…I wish my husband/wife or fiancé would _____more. Explain.

4. What ways can I show love more in my marriage or relationship?

5. What things do you do for your spouse/fiancé that shows *your* love for your spouse? (this shows what you "think" would please your spouse.) Does it?

6. What generational issues need to be dealt with in your family line? Spouse's family line? Discuss this together and pray appropriately as in this chapter.

4

Advice

1. No such word as DIVORCE

Set your heart and mind with the fact that **divorce is not an option**! I will repeat this. From the start, set your mind and heart that divorce is NOT an option. It is not God's way and it is not your way. Solving the problem, whatever it is, is the option. Whatever the world throws our way, whatever the enemy throws our way, getting through it is the only option. Finding our way through the difficult situation; finding the solution. Not giving up! This goes against the grain of society. We live in a quick fix society and divorce is not a quick fix. People get deeply hurt and children get deeply wounded as well. Sometimes you may even hear the enemy scream the words divorce to you, but recognize where it is coming from. "For better or worse," means <u>working at it</u> and loving each other through good times and difficult times…better or worse, richer or poorer, sickness and in health, even when it is hard to find the solution, even when it's hard to *feel* the love you once had. None of us knows what lies ahead, but I can guarantee you that you will go through hard times. Know it. Expect it, and be ready! We all do. Don't be surprised when it comes.

"Dear friends, don't be surprised at the fiery trials you are going through, as if something strange were happening to you." 1 Peter 4:12. "Dear brothers and sisters, when trouble comes your way, consider it an opportunity for great joy. For you know that when your faith is tested, your endurance has a chance to grow. So let it grow for when your endurance is fully developed, you will be perfect and complete, needing nothing." James 1:2-4.

Of course some go through harder trials than others but it is what we do with them when they come. You will get through them. Hard times come and hard times go; you get through them together. Look to God and keep praising the Lord. I have heard of many instances when a terrible crisis comes and instead of husband and wife coming together to be support for each other, it wrecks the marriage. This should not be. Not only should it strengthen the marriage and draw us closer together, but as we see in the scriptures it should make us more Christ-like. It should perfect us to become more complete in Him. Our faith is tested and our faith becomes stronger.

In over 36 years of marriage, there have been times that I just really thought we would never make it through. I gave up and threw in the towel. You may lose hope, you may lose love, you may lose trust, you may seem to lose bonds and not even care. It just takes one person, one of you, to fight to save the marriage. It can be done in the hardest of hard times, only with God. I repeat, ONLY with God. He is a God of miracles. Sometimes that is what it takes...a miracle. Many know what I am talking about. Some may not have any idea, but it is my prayer that you will be able to use this information in time of need. Pray! God is on your side. Maybe this is why it is His will that we marry in His presence so He is the center of our marriage. He knows we need Him and really cannot do it without Him.

According to former witches and satanists, there are many satanists and witches praying and fasting for divorce in marriages and for families to be broken, especially Christian marriages. Know that your problems may not be all of your issues, but there are spiritual forces against us. That does not mean you are fighting a losing battle; He who is in you is greater. We have our Creator, the Living God on our side. He loves marriage and loves close families. He knows that it is the family unit that strengthens and nurtures healthy children and parents. This is why the enemy attacks the family unit.

If this is not your first marriage and your ex-husband or ex-wife is married to another, there are sacred bonds between the two of you. You may think, "I wouldn't want them back." Even so, you are not as disconnected as you might think. No man can separate it and surely not a piece of paper that says divorce.

"You cry out, "Why doesn't the Lord accept my worship?" I'll tell you why! Because the Lord witnessed the vows you and your wife made when you were young. But you have been unfaithful to her, though she remained your faithful partner, the wife of your marriage vows."

"Didn't the Lord make you one with your wife? In body and spirit you are His. And what does He want? He desires Godly children from your union. So guard your heart; remain loyal to the wife of your youth. **For I hate divorce, says the Lord, the God of Israel.** To divorce your wife is to overwhelm her with cruelty, says the Lord of Heaven's Armies. "So guard your heart; do not be unfaithful to your wife." Malachi 12-16. Be faithful... Stay faithful to your husband and to your wife.

Marriage is a sacred covenant between you and your spouse and God. You make a vow for life. It is an agreement before God, a promise binding and sacred like that of God for His people. God established marriage for us. It is good for us. Keep prayer in your marriage, stay close to God, and stay in the Word. You need strength to get through the rough spots of life; whether they affect your marriage or they don't, you still need God.

Individual or Group Questions

1. In what areas do I feel the enemy is coming against our marriage or family?

2. Discuss together and make a list together in what areas in your lives the enemy is coming against you and your marriage and family. Then pray together as a couple, in Jesus' Name, against the powers of the enemy against your relationship, marriage, and family. Take up the authority you have in Jesus.

2. Communication

I believe communication is one of the most important key elements of marriage. This is what I tell those who ask me for advice. Without healthy communication, not only will our relationship suffer emotionally but our sexual relationship will die as well. God created women to need communication in order for all the other aspects of our relationship to flow freely. All stems from the health of the communication element of the relationship. The relationship thrives from this. Communication needs to stay open and flow freely. Don't close up. Guard against this, because this is an area where the enemy will come in and attack. This can be difficult when some people have a problem opening up and sharing and are naturally closed.

Remember how you had to be open in the early part of the relationship of getting to know one another. Know that this needs to continue for your marriage to continue to be healthy and growing. Nothing hurts more than being closed out. It is where you will have to stretch yourself if it is not your way to be open. Of course if it is your way be open and talkative, be careful of talking too much. Just to be talking on and on or talking at people and your spouse is a turn off. This will drive your spouse nuts and cause him/her to build a wall to shut you out.

Remember to ask, "How was your day today?" Care how the other's day was. It is healthy at times, too, to just be in each other's company and just "be"... Just be content in the presence of your loved one. It reminds me a Normal Rockwell painting with an elderly couple in rocking chairs with their spouse of many years, and they are content; she knitting and he reading a paper, peace in the quiet. They're just content and happy being together; a silent communication. We should be content just "being" with our life mate too. Also there should be times of comfort, cuddling and loving as you had before marriage; this is keeping the romance in the marriage, and this is important too. It should not stop just because you are married or old and married many years. It is not just up to the man, or not just up to the woman, to keep the romance in the marriage; both men and women need this.

Many men are not always talkers and can tend to be of few words. I did not have this problem; my husband loves to talk, but for those who are not open or talkative, you will need to stretch your self, and talk more. Possibly some men and women need to stretch themselves to talk less. You do need to communicate good things and your problems. Without communication you will not have a leg to stand on in marriage. If there is a problem, you need to lovingly share it with your beloved as your best friend. Take it to God and pray together about it. You must share; otherwise, they will have no idea what the problem is or even if there is a problem. Work at the problems and care! Work at it until you find a solution, even if it is uncomfortable or is even painful. Work at your marriage. DO NOT TAKE EACH OTHER FOR GRANTED! And just because there are problems does not mean you are not meant for each other; it means there are areas you in which need to work a little harder at. Now and then this will happen to everyone. After many years of marriage it is easy to take each other for granted. Guard against this.

No marriage is perfect and without any problems. All strong marriages got that way because each problem that arose was dealt with and not ignored. Ignoring a problem will not make a problem go away but it will make the problem grow. Care where the other is unhappy; most often you are the one who can take care of that need or at least support the other in his/her trials.

Many times it is hard for our egos that we are not perfect. It is hard to accept that we may even be the cause of our spouse's pain. If it helps, none of us is perfect. Part of being married is learning how to fulfill each other's needs. We should not be demanding but naturally caring and loving about one another.

Learn about your spouse; ask about his or her likes and dislikes. It is fun to learn more about our life mate. That never ends because we all are ever changing and growing, at least we should be. This will benefit your relationship and keep it fresh and exciting. Doing random loving things keeps things fresh and exciting too! It fans the flame of romance.

Individual or Group Questions

1. In what areas do I need to open up and share with my spouse or fiancé? What areas am I uncomfortable sharing?

2. In what areas might I be the cause of stress and problems in my relationship? What can I do to alleviate this?

3. Answer this question for your spouse/fiancé. I wish you knew this about me?

3. Hard Times will come and go

You will have hard times. You will have disagreements and disappointments but know they will pass. This is part of life. There is nothing you cannot get through with each other, especially with God. God is the marriage saver. He helps you in time of need. When it seems nothing can save it, but by the grace of God, a marriage can be saved. His grace sustains us.

"You have heard the law that says, a man can divorce his wife by merely giving her a written notice of divorce. But I say that a man, who divorces his wife, unless she has been unfaithful, causes her to commit adultery. And anyone who marries a divorced woman also commits adultery." Matt 5:31. In other words your vows are binding till one dies. Being unfaithful seems to break that vow but I have seen over and over again, God saves broken marriages, even when adultery has taken place. As in Malachi 2, we see that God says, "don't divorce" and "I hate divorce." Whether adultery is your reason or not for wanting to divorce, God renews and forgives and so can we. Not everything is acceptable, but everything is forgivable. It's best to stay away from sin because it is extremely painful, but all sin is forgivable. Forgive so you will be forgiven.

I once saw a good couple we loved so dearly, divorce; it was a bitter divorce. One became very bitter and it transformed that one into a hard-hearted person of bitterness. Never smiling, the bitterness took over that person's whole being even years later. I would try to make this one smile because this person just couldn't, as if they might break. It hurt my friend to smile. This is what bitterness can do; it takes root and affects our whole being. Strangely enough, I was reading the book, *Divine Revelation of Hell*.[6] The Lord continuously took the author, Mary Baxter, to visit hell with Him during her prayer time. She met many people and saw what they were experiencing in hell.

They met this woman in hell who had divorced and through it allowed bitterness to get into her heart and take over her. She had been a Christian woman and the bitterness turned her heart away from God. We cannot hold on to things. It's best to let go before thoughts of divorce and return to the love we had when we first began. If that is too late and you have already remarried, please let go of all bitterness and forgive.

God renews love and trust in marriages that are seemingly lost forever, even when you think you can never get over what the other has said or done. There is nothing unforgivable. If hearts are turned to God, He will save all marriages. That is His heart! He renews hearts and heals the wounds. You must not let the root of bitterness get into your hearts.

Forgiveness is important for a healthy life in all areas. Unforgiveness is the root of many diseases. There isn't anything we cannot get through. It may hurt for a time until it is healed. There is no wound Jesus cannot heal. By all that appears, it may look like the marriage is over, but with God all things are possible. I pray you hear these words in time of need. Communication is so important. It may hurt to communicate when there are misunderstandings or disagreements. It may hurt to hear you are half the problem, but as much as it hurts, healing takes place with God's grace when we talk it out. I pray for the day when divorce is lowering in the Body of Christ rather than rising in America! The best remedy is to stay close to your Father God. He is the answer!

"Some Pharisees came and tried to trap Him with this question; "Should a man be allowed to divorce his wife for just any reason? Jesus replied, Haven't you read the Scriptures? "Have you not read that He who created them from the beginning made them male and female, and said, 'Therefore a man shall leave his father and his mother and hold fast to his wife, and the two shall become one flesh?" "So they are no longer two but one flesh. What God has joined together, let no man separate." They said to him, "Why then did Moses command one to give a certificate of divorce and to send her away?" He said to them, "Because of your hardness of heart Moses allowed you to divorce your wives, but from the beginning it was not so. And I say to you: whoever divorces his wife, except for sexual immorality, and marries, commits adultery." Matt 19:3.

"What God has joined together let no man separate." Mark 10:39. What God joins together, even if you think a man can separate; truly only God can do the separating.

Does our hard heart give us right to divorce? Apparently it does. I hope so, because there is so much divorce in our society today, but it is not God's will for us. I remember in the late 70s, when I moved to California, I was shocked at how much more divorce was there than in New York. Now in the 2000s, there is so much more divorce everywhere than that time, even prominent spiritual leaders and pastors in the body of Christ. I believe all who are divorced are in some way spiritually connected to their first husband or wife.

Another point is that God does not want to give a certificate of divorce, Jesus said this. He wills for you to make it through. He knows that once you get through the rough times, it will be better on the other side. Apparently sexual immorality breaks the vow or God will break the vow for that reason. Sexual immorality defiles the person and causes him/her to become impure. It may be for the protection of the innocent spouse. It is a doorway for demons to come in and causes one to defile a spouse when they come together in union. We have seen that play out in the physical, by people bringing sexually transmitted diseases home to their spouse; spiritually this defiles as well. In spite of this, I have seen many marriages survive adultery and have seen God restore and purify both people through love, forgiveness, prayer with lots of communication and God's grace. It can be a difficult process but it is worth it.

The question would be when Jesus said, "What God has joined together, let no man separate." Did God join you together; was it His will? Were you meant to be together, or was it a mistake from the start? We all make mistakes at times. It needs to be taken to God Himself; press into Him for an answer. But I do believe that there is forgiveness for everything. Our God is a forgiving God even though He hates divorce. He hates the hurtful effects on us.

The Bible gives an indication of what constitutes a marriage. When is it that God seals that marriage? Let us look at the marriage of Jacob and Rachel and Leah. This shows us something. First why did God allow men to marry more than one wife? It was because of their hardened hearts. I have been told by an old friend who was raised by a father who had two wives in the Mormon community out west that often one wife is favored, and it is sad for the other. In this situation, his mother was the elder and the less favored wife.

We all know the story of Jacob and Rachel. In Genesis 20:21-30, Jacob loved Rachel so much and wanted to marry her. They were betrothed, and he worked for her father for 7 years in order for her father to give them permission. When the seven years was completed, Rachel's father had the marriage feast, a celebration. This all was with Rachel; the betrothal, the dowry, the 7 years, and the marriage feast. Now came the time for the wedding night. "But that night, when it was dark, Laban took Leah to Jacob, and he slept with her. But when Jacob woke up in the morning – it was Leah!" Genesis 29:23 & 25. Now look at this, in verse 26, "A week after Jacob had *married* Leah, Laban gave him Rachel too." Now he had already been betrothed, Jacob worked 7 years for Rachel, and he already had a marriage celebration with Rachel, but he was married to Leah because they had lain with each other. It was in the consummation that marriage took place.

Now-a-days the vows too are binding and we also see in Ezekiel 18:8 it is the marriage vows and covenant which pronounced Israel married to God. "I wrapped my cloak around you to cover your nakedness and declared my marriage vows. I made a covenant with you, says the Sovereign Lord, and you became mine."

When we make vows to our loved ones, it is a covenant. What is a covenant? A covenant is an unconditional promise. Webster's Collegiate Dictionary says it is "a promise, pledge or contract." "A formal, solemn, and binding contract."[7] Don't forget this was done under God.

What is a vow? Again, Webster's Collegiate Dictionary says, a vow is "a solemn promise, in which a person binds himself to an act, service or condition. To bind or consecrate by a vow. To promise solemnly. To swear."[8] Again I remind you this was done for most in the presence of, and to, God as well as to your husband or wife. The vow was made in the natural and in the spiritual.

Prayers for Divorced People

Break the ungodly soul ties between you and your past spouse(s). Forgive everything that needs to be forgiven so that bitterness is not carried throughout your life or take root in your heart.

Repent for the wrong you have done in the marriage and forgive yourself for the wrong you have done.

You also need to repent for breaking the past marriage vow(s) and covenant(s). Renounce the vow in Jesus' Name. Do this for each marriage vow that was broken. Ask the Lord to break the vow for you, since no man can do this. Ask the Lord to cleanse you in the Blood of the Lamb of all of this.

Ask the Lord to cleanse you of any defilement that came upon you because of any adultery that you or your spouse may have committed, and repent for any physical, mental or verbal abuse committed, or break off what was received. If there was any verbal abuse, nullify all negative words spoken to you, about you and over you. Break any curses spoken over you. Cover yourself with the Precious Blood of Jesus. Ask the Lord to break any natural and spiritual repercussions and curses because of the divorce(s), broken covenant and broken vows, In Jesus' Name. Renounce all ungodly soul ties with each ex-spouse. Renounce that ungodly soul tie and ask God to break it in Jesus' Name. Amen.

Remember God is the only one who can break the marriage bonds that He bound.

Are all marriages bound by God?

In Ezra 9 & 10 we learn there was a time when God was angry about the marriages between His people and the pagans, which God called a terrible sin. He called the marriages, "a terrible sin." We see that those people were married, but God had not blessed those marriages, and He even commanded they leave their families right away and made them vow to divorce. This is an example of a time when God did not bless these marriages and it even made Him very angry. Because of the sin of marrying pagan women, their sin came upon them and spread rapidly throughout God's people. It is important to God that we stay pure, and if we marry impure people it defiles us. I also do not believe God would bind together or bless the marriages of homosexuals. Why? It doesn't matter what I think or feel; we need to look at the word of God. That is the light to guide our feet and a light for our path. Leviticus 18 has a list of forbidden sexual practices which are perverse and detestable to the Lord.

"Do not practice homosexuality, having sex with another man as with a woman. It is a detestable sin." Lev. 18:22. Not just a sin but a detestable sin. What does detestable mean? The Dictionary says it is an intense dislike, extreme hatred or contempt, loathing, curse.[9] So if God was to bind the two men or two women together, He would be sinning by doing so. God does not sin, so He could not bless or bind two homosexuals together.

"If a man practices homosexuality, having sex with another man as with a woman, both men have

108

committed a detestable act. They must both be put to death, for they are guilty of a capital offense." Lev. 20:13. I have to wonder if we are subjecting ourselves and our country to the judgment of God by promoting homosexual practice, by legalizing homosexual marriage.

Again, in the New Testament, "Don't you realize that those who do wrong will not inherit the Kingdom of God? Don't fool yourselves. Those who indulge in sexual sin, or who worship idols, or commit adultery, or are male prostitutes, or practice homosexuality, or are thieves, or greedy people, or drunkards, or are abusive, or cheat people - none of these will inherit the Kingdom of God. Some of you were once like that. But you were cleansed; you were made holy; you were made right with God by calling on the name of the Lord Jesus Christ and by the Spirit of our God." 1 Corinthians 6:9-11.

"The law is for people who are sexually immoral, or who practice homosexuality, or are slave traders, liars, promise breakers, who do anything else that contradicts the wholesome teaching that comes from the glorious Good News entrusted to me by our blessed God." 1 Timothy 1:10.

Homosexuality took over the men of Sodom and Gomorrah and God destroyed the whole city. I say all this to show that there are times when God does not bind a marriage together. Many Christian homosexual couples and churches vow to God, but did He bring them together? I do not believe so. Never in the Bible did God say he allowed homosexuality because of hardness of hearts, or for any reason. No, actually we see He literally destroyed a city because of it. We never saw God allow babies to be killed because of hardness of hearts, but we do see where God did allow divorce because of hardness of hearts, even though it was not His will or first choice for His people.

Divorce is not the unforgivable sin; everyone can be forgiven their sins when they repent and turn from their sin. Jesus said when the adulterous was caught, "Go and sin no more."

I have had a person call me to tell me that they told "so and so" they are going to hell because they are divorced. We do not know each person's personal situation unless we have walked in their shoes. Jesus said in the case of the adulterous, "He who has no sin, cast the first stone." Jesus caused a lot of men to drop their stones and walk away. He said this even though it was written in the Word to stone such people.

We know God's heart on divorce. He hates it. But He forgives if we full-heartedly repent. Do not condemn yourself or anyone else. I know many reading this book have been divorced so this is why I am adding this. I am not condoning divorce. It hurts people. Be sure you are marrying the right person, the one God has chosen. Put yourself in a position to hear the voice of God. I was only 18 and not even born again and I heard the will of the Lord to marry my husband. So can you. My main point in this book is that marriages can be saved but many are already into second and third marriages. Let's try to save those by getting healed and becoming the best we can be.

"Let us now make a covenant with our God to divorce our pagan wives and to send them away with their children. We will follow the advice given by you and by the others who respect the commands of our God." Ezra 10:3.

"So now confess your sin to the Lord, the God of your ancestors, and do what He demands. Separate yourselves from the people of the land and from these pagan women." Ezra 10:11.

If you are married to a person who does detestable things, you may be beaten and/or cursed daily and abused. Perhaps someone tricked you to think a person was one way and turned out to be totally the opposite because of deceit. I would wonder if that was God's will for you. It is not for me to say whether God has blessed that marriage. But I do see a time in scriptures when God commanded His people to separate from sinful people and called for them to divorce. I can not judge.

"You must not intermarry with them. Do not let your daughters and sons marry their sons and daughters, for they will lead your children away from me to worship other gods. Then the anger of the Lord will burn against you and He will quickly destroy you." Deut. 7:3-4. This shows that the sin in the life of your spouse can overtake you if the other's life has gone bad. In other words, your spouse can be going to hell and drag you there with him/her. These are special circumstances, not the average marriage. Nowadays there is more and more of this happening as the days get more evil.

Remember Exodus 22:10; were you being loved, nurtured as you both vowed? Or did you or your spouse break your vows and are guilty of neglect? I do believe there is redemption for many people. I believe there are instances where God pardons and forgives. He is a very loving and forgiving God. But with all your heart and strength, every measure should be taken to save your marriage. I am giving tools in this book that will help, Such as by praying off the enemy and other ways to nurture and strengthen your marriage and seek God with all your mind, heart, and strength. Get prayer counseling, go get inner healing. You would never regret it, and it would make not only your marriage better and stronger but your entire life would be blessed by it, as well as all the generations after you.

Prayers for Breaking Things from Past Marriages

A. First Repent for all the wrong you did in the past marriage(s). We all do wrong; it is rare, if ever, that it is all one person's fault even when it looks one sided. We must acknowledge the wrong we did.

B. Repent for Divorce; God hates divorce. **We also see in scripture that He also hates for us to marry ungodly and pagan people. You may need to repent for this. Or you may need to repent for marrying in rebellion.** Were you living a rebellious lifestyle at the time? This will put you in the wrong place at the wrong time, with the wrong people. If this is appropriate, ask the Lord and follow the Holy Spirit on what fits with your particular situation. If you are not married yet it is not too late to stop it before you make the mistake.

C. Ask God to break all the ungodly, unhealthy soul ties with your ex-husband or ex-wife. Ask God to break the ties that He bound and to separate the oneness between the two of you that you might be walking in, in Jesus' Name.

I have heard the testimony of someone who heard from the Lord; He had the person repent for the sin of marrying in rebellion. If this individual weren't in rebellion, she would not have married the wrong person, so her greatest sin was rebellion; she was regularly beaten and abused while married.

I find interesting a couple of statements from Jesus in the midst of His strong words about divorce in

Matthew 19. First, God did permit divorce because of the hard hearts of the people in the past. It was not His will but He allowed it. It was not the way He created it to be. It was not this way in the beginning.

In the NIV the Pharisees asked, "Is it lawful for a man to divorce his wife for any and every reason." Matthew 19:3. We must understand that the Pharisees were out to trick him. Basically men were just putting away their wives for "any and every" reason.

Jesus revealed God's true heart about divorce. It is better to not remarry. But in the end, in Matthew 19:11, "Not everyone can accept this statement, Jesus said, "Only those whom God helps." Your marriage can be saved with God's help. I know many people's testimonies of this. And if you decide not to marry or remarry, God will help those who choose this way.

In the end of verse 11, "Let anyone accept this who can." I have to believe God is the same yesterday, today and tomorrow. He will forgive divorce as He did in the scriptures during Moses' time. But my advice to you is to not have a hard heart like they had in Moses' time. It got them into a lot of hardships because of it. Forty years of needless wandering because of their rebellion. Soften your heart and give in some with your spouse; change some to make your marriage work. It takes changes on both the man and the woman's part. Both are acting out in reaction to the other's actions and decisions. Maybe some of your stubbornness is causing or promoting trouble in your marriage. That would be your sin, the sin of stubbornness, which is a hard heart. Often we do not see our own stubbornness, only the other person's. We often times miss our own sinfulness and shortcomings when viewing our partner's sin against us. We justify our actions because of what we see coming against us.

I guarantee both sides sin. We all sin and fall short of the Glory of God.

Pray that God forgives your past divorce as He did in the scriptures. Our God is a loving and forgiving God. Go humbly to Him with repentance. Talk to Him, He will talk to you.

If you are finding that you are divorcing over and over you may need inner healing. Possibly you continuously keep choosing the same type of person who is dysfunctional, violent, abusive, an alcoholic, or other negative issues. If this is the case you need to realize you are worth better than this. Don't choose people who are bad for you. Love and respect yourself enough to raise your standard.

Maybe the marriages could have been saved with a little more work. Maybe your spouse gave up the marriage and you would have persevered to save it. There are so many reasons why marriages are brought to an end. Many times it is out of your control.

In My life, when my marriage seemed to be taking a nose dive and heading for divorce, we turned to God and sought God together with humble and broken hearts. If you do this, God saves. Pray together and read the scriptures together, and exchange your heart of stone for a new, soft and open heart. If you don't, you are liable to have the same problems in your second marriage as you did in the first.

NLT Ephesians 5:21 says, "And further, submit to one another out of reverence for Christ. Wives, this means submit to your husbands as to the Lord. A husband is the head of his wife as Christ is the head of the church. He is the Savior of His Body, the Church. As the church submits to Christ, so you wives should submit to your husbands in everything." This means ladies that you may stand your ground and even argue your case, but in the end you must submit to your husband. It surely is not hard to submit when you are being treated special, like Jesus loves us and the church. It is a blessing to submit. Both submit to one another.

"Husbands, this means love your wives, just as Christ loved the church. He gave up his life for her; to make her holy and clean, washed by the cleansing of God's word. He did this to present her to himself as a glorious church without a spot or wrinkle or any other blemish. Instead, she will be holy and without fault. In the same way, husbands ought to love their wives as they love their own bodies. A man who loves his wife actually shows love for himself. No one hates his own body but feeds and cares for it, just as Christ cares for the church. And we are members of His body." Ephesians 5:25-30.

This means, men, that she may disagree at times and she may be right or not right, but that you need to respect and discern. You must listen with your heart as you would want to be heard, treated, loved and cared for. She is not always right and you are not always right. Never lead your family out of stubbornness but by the grace of God. He should be leading and you following Him. A great leader is a great follower of God. God is the head.

Marriage is made up of two people, and both need to confirm decisions between each other, especially when they are big decisions. No big decisions should ever be made without the other's knowledge or input. It is a way to confirm the decision. If one is against something, I would seek God again through prayer. Tell God that "if" it is His will, to change the other's heart; He will do it and it will then be confirmed to you. God will make His will known; ultimately it is His decision, not the husband's or wives. What does God say? In our experience God will let you both know, not just one. If the wife is against something strongly, it should be a check in your spirit and, you, husband, should seek God further. When the time is right, He will let you both know.

For example, once when we were moving, I knew months before from God that we were to move. I did not know when or where, but I knew we were moving. My husband did not know and was even strongly against moving. When God told me we were moving, I told God if we move, it has to be done all through my husband, Mike. God did just that; He worked through Mike on the timing and the location of the move. His feet were firmly planted in the soil of his family's land and we were living in the house that he labored to build with his own hands. No one could move him but God. And that is just what God did. In God's time! So we must trust that God works through each other. God moved Mike in due time, and I had to trust the time and the place we were moving to. I did not want to move to Branson, but I submitted to my husband and trusted he heard from God as to where we were to move. See, God used us both and confirmed through us both. If one is firmly against something, then we need to check with God and make sure it is not from our own heart. God is the head; God is the leader of our marriage, family, and our life.

"Do to others whatever you would like them to do to you. This is the essence of all that is taught in the law and the prophets." NLT Matthew 7:12. This means absolutely no abuse in any way, verbal, physical or sexual. This goes for the wife to the husband as well as husband to wife; compromise, which is to give and take and not be controlling. One is never always right, and one is never always wrong. Your job, husbands, is to love and cherish, guide, protect and try to understand. Both should strive to keep the peace. Both should stay close to God. "God blesses the humble for they will inherit the whole earth." Matthew 5:5. "Blessed are the peace makers." Matthew 5:9.

One reason many get upset in a marriage is because they don't feel heard, loved, or cared about. It is important to make sure that your spouse is not taken for granted and knows he or she is loved, cherished and heard. You may not always agree, but you at least listen and hear each other's wants, needs and views. Come to a middle ground; many don't get this. They start demanding to be heard. It becomes a push and pull reaction, each becomes demanding to be important and demanding to be heard. Some people shrink away and lose their identity.

Both need to strive to keep the romance in the marriage. Continue to romance each other. Remember this too...everyone needs a loving touch. Nobody can go through life without a hug. Don't let go of these things. It is important to have quality time and affection, and this affection needs to pour out of us onto the children. They, too, need pure and affectionate touch; it is a fact that children cannot grow normally without it, and it should never be taken for granted. Everyone needs love and the feeling of importance. Not everyone has gotten this and this is why we have a dysfunctional world. No child or adult should go a day without a hug.

Husbands, many women need to hear, "I love you," and most need a hug daily or a gentle loving touch. Wives, many men need to hear, "I love you" too. It is essential that you communicate and talk daily. Both need unconditional love. Women, it is essential that you honor and respect your husbands; build up, don't nag or tear down. Men need respect. Many times women can nag and tear down a man with their tongue. I once knew a couple and the man would beat his wife. Everyone thought it was terrible and of course it was. But what nobody knew is that he was beaten just as badly by her with her tongue. Men need to respect and honor their wives as well. The tongue is the quickest way to treat one another with honor, love, respect and blessings.

Jude verse 20 says, "But you, dear friends must build each other up in your most holy faith, pray in the power of the Holy Spirit." This begins at home; all we learn in the scriptures, we need to practice at home. I can't stress this enough. It can't only be practiced in front of people or neighbors. What we do behind closed doors will be exposed. If you only do it out in front of people, you are a hypocrite; you must love and honor and bless in your homes first. Our true character is proven in the home.

Often we notice and speak out about the negative each other does; let's speak out and notice the good the other does.

So many people seem like normal people, but if you had any clue of what was happening to people in the secret places in their homes you would cringe. Children, husbands and wives are abused verbally, physically, sexually, and emotionally, some severely. Parents are being abused by their kids or teens. This should never be, but I've learned it happens often. The enemy attacks in the home and often in Christian homes. Nobody even knows it yet they go to our churches, serve in our churches, and some even pastor our churches. We see them at work and they are in classes at schools with our children. We know them and even like them. They look like nice families, and they hide behind a smile. I've met many of them and my heart breaks for them. God's people need healing! That is part of the reason for writing this book.

"Keep putting into practice all you learned and received from me – everything you've heard from me and saw me doing. Then the God of peace will be with you." Philippians 4:9.

Individual or Group Questions

1. What areas are my weak points in my character? Take a character check.

2. In what way do I need more affection from my spouse/fiancé?

3. Do I feel heard by my spouse/finance'? In what areas or ways do I need to hear better?

4. Do I feel heard by my spouse/fiancé? In what areas or ways do they need to hear me better?

5. What is a vow? What is a marriage covenant? What does this mean to me?

4. Controlling Your Tongue

James chapter 3 has a lot to say about controlling the tongue. When you have something mean to say, practice "holding your tongue." It speaks of the tongue being a flame of fire. And a tiny spark can start a great forest fire. What you say can defile yourself and others and it can cause you to sin. Your tongue can be full of deadly poison. And what you say comes from the heart, and sometimes our heart can sound pretty evil. Sometimes we bless with our tongue, and sometimes we curse with the same tongue. We need to guard what we say and speak positively. When we speak negatively, it becomes curses and we don't even realize it, spewing all over everyone and our own self. "The tongue has the power of life and death." Proverb 18:21.

A word has to come to our thoughts first before it turns to sin, when we speak it or turn it into a negative action which is sin. We need to keep negative thoughts out and then they won't pass through our tongues. This goes for when we are around the children as well. They learn what they hear. If you show love, respect and are patient, they will learn it. If you are negative, judging and condemning, they will learn this too. They are like sponges and learn quickly from their environment. If you teach anger, disrespect, and abuse, they pick that right up. When you sow seeds of anger, disrespect, abuse and such negative reactions, they will come back to you.

Try to agree with your spouse when it comes to the children and disciplining them. Don't argue about it in front of the kids, but be in agreement and follow through with what you say. That doesn't mean never ever break what you say, but follow through with consistency. The best way to teach your children love, honor and respect is to treat them that way. Just because they are young does not mean they don't deserve your respect; they are God's creation and very special.

Often times what happens is that we can guard our mouths when we are out around other people, but when we are home we let it all fall out. This should not be. Those whom we live with are very special, and we want our children to grow up in a pure and holy home. So we need to guard our home and guard what comes out of our mouths to edify, build up, strengthen and bless our husband, wife and children. Speak only what is loving, honorable, pure and kind. This is to not ignore problems, but we should discuss them before they become mountains or shouting matches. This also teaches our children self control.

"Anyone who loves to quarrel loves sin." Proverb 17:19. "For God is working in you, giving you the desire and the power to do what pleases Him. Do everything without complaining and arguing so that no one can criticize you. Live clean, innocent lives as children of God, shining like bright lights in a world full of crooked and perverse people." Philippians 2:13-15.

"The earnest prayer of a righteous person has great power and produces results." James 5:16. If we are fighting all the time, how powerful might our prayers be? "The one who guards his mouth preserves his life; the one who opens wide his lips come to ruins." Proverb 13:3.

"If you claim to be religious but don't control your tongue, you are fooling yourself, and your religion is worthless." James 1:26.

We just don't realize that words are powerful and can make or break someone. God created the world with His words. There is energy in words, a force that is either positive or negative. If you speak negatively long enough to someone, not only are you hurting yourself but hurting and cursing others, especially when anger or insult is behind it. That is a negative energy going forth from your lips and heart. You can curse your own life and your own family's lives by speaking negatively. There is a backlash. As Christians our words have power, especially prophetic people. When we speak negatively to people, it has a very strong and lasting impact. Then we are working for and being used by the enemy rather than for the Lord, and we don't even know it. We must watch our tongue.

You have a choice; fix your eyes on what is good and honorable, or follow the evil intentions of the heart and flesh. Move by the flesh or by the Spirit. The enemy works through our flesh and God works through the spirit. How do we fix our eyes on what is good? Our family has good and bad, but we should fix our eyes on the good in them. Do we want people just looking and focusing on the bad in us? Jesus said that how we judge is how we will be judged.

We all have good and bad qualities. When we focus on the negative, it tends to grow larger or appears larger than it really is. It is an illusion. It becomes exaggerated in our minds. Choose to see good in people; this honors people. Satan would have us focus on the shortcomings of people, especially of our spouse, because those shortcomings grow and grow larger than they really are and that causes trouble. If done long enough, it becomes a bad habit and negative way of life to only see negative. This can be the negative in people or negative in situations. So catch yourself and see what your mind is focusing on.

There may be one negative thing and an abundance of good, but we can let that one negative thing look greater than all the good. Remember they have to overlook our negative too. Don't get into the habit of seeing the negative of life; that steals your joy. If you find you are continuously looking at the negative and grumbling and complaining all the time, there is a problem. God has wonderful promises for those who love Him. Let's enjoy life to the fullest and not let satan steal our joy of life.

If you grew up under negativity, forgive now those who were negative towards you before you do the same. If you picked it up from someone, forgive that person, fight the enemy on this and get your joy back. It is hard to live with someone who is negative all the time. It is not of God but of the enemy. Begin to look at the positive in life. Especially in these end times there is a lot of negative out there, but the positive thing to do is pray and not complain. Prayer changes things! Take action against the wrong that is taking place; don't just sit back and complain. Pray! When you stay close to God, you will not be dwelling on negative. Our God is not a condemning God. He is love, peace and kindness. So if you find condemnation in your speech, know that is not of God and you may need a healing. It is good to do regular checks on yourself.

Prayer for Walking in Condemnation and Negativity

Remember, if you grew up under condemnation then you most likely judged your parent for this. You need to first repent for judging them and for your own condemnation that you've walked in and the negativity, then forgive them. Renounce the judgment and break the sowing and reaping process off your life, in Jesus Name. Bind

up any negative spirits that have taken up residence in or on you, in Jesus Name. Cast them out in Jesus Name. Ask God to teach you how to be loving and positive with your words and attitude.

Choose to speak uplifting, good, and positive things to your family. If you are called stupid enough times, you will believe it; when you believe it, you become what you believe. If a young girl who is very ugly is called beautiful by her father, she believes she is beautiful. If a beautiful girl is called ugly and treated ugly her whole life, it doesn't matter how beautiful she is, she will believe and feel that she is ugly. I have seen this. We must compliment with kind uplifting words in our homes. We are accountable for every word we speak.

I have known some of the most beautiful young women who just cannot believe they are beautiful because their fathers never affirmed them, or made them feel beautiful, special or important. Validate your children. They are important, so let's make them feel important. It begins with you...their mother and father. Sons see how you treat their mother. If you, as the father, treat their mother poorly, so will they treat her that way, and they will also treat their wives that way. If you, as the mother, treat their father poorly, your daughters too will have no respect for their father or husbands. It is a ripple effect. Teach respect for each other in the family. Each person counts and so does each one's thoughts.

This scripture shows how serious this is when Jesus says, in Matthew 12:36, "And I tell you this, you must give an account on judgment day for every idle word you speak. The words you say will either acquit you or condemn you." (Some scriptures say "thoughtless" words and some say "careless" words. We must take this seriously.

When my children were little, we had some words that were not allowed to be said to one another. Of course some were the obvious swear words but also the typical words or phrases like "stupid," "you idiot," "you're dumb," "I hate you," and other negative and hurtful words. That meant that we, too, could not call them or anyone those words either. That kept us accountable as well. We couldn't do what we told the kids they couldn't do. It helped bring peace into the home.

Think of what an impact we can have on our families and the world with our tongues, by our words. When times are hard, we can speak into people's lives by speaking uplifting and positive words---kind, loving, gentle words. We are each God's mouthpiece. We must watch not only what, but how, we speak. Several times I heard a mother say to her grown son, "You are going to get cancer just like your father." It was said with impact. It felt like a fireball being sent through the air. People have no idea what they are doing with their words. When I hear words that are curses, even if the person realizes it or not, I say a quick short prayer to counteract them. It is good to do this. Bind those words up and nullify them in Jesus Name. Proverb 4:20 says words penetrate deep into the heart. Let us give out good, positive and godly words to bring life, healing and wholeness. When we speak good, wholesome and positive, loving words it too will penetrate deep into the heart. Think of this when talking to our family who we seed into daily. If we continue to speak negatively we ourselves will become negative and a challenge to be around.

Prayer against Negative Words

I cast every negative word to the ground that was spoken to me or over me or behind my back. I nullify every curse and negative word, in Jesus' Name. I take every knife out of my back, in Jesus' Name, and cast them all to the ground. I render them all powerless, in the Mighty Name of Jesus. Cover me with the Precious Blood of Jesus. Thank you Lord. Amen. Lord take every negative word and seed that has penetrated deep in my heart and take them out and cleanse any residue from my heart. In Jesus' Name, Amen.

Can you imagine that we are working "for" satan when we speak negatively? If you are Christian or not, you are being used by the enemy when you speak and act negatively. We must stop working for the enemy and stop speaking death. We often say over and over, "I have no money," "I'm always lacking," and "I am poor." We keep declaring negative over our lives. Speak what we do not see as if it were. We must stop cursing ourselves and others. We are children of God, and we are to speak life with our tongues. We should not ridicule, embarrass, tear down or attack our husband, wife, children or anyone, especially if we have authority over people in any way. I strongly feel this is so important, and that is why I am spending time with this. If you can do this simple thing, your family you will be blessed and your future generations will be blessed. See the good and declare the good in people. Think of this, our children for the first 5 years of their life are basically around only their family. You have the power and control to seed good and godly things into them. If you only sow negative and tear them down then that is what they become. They become a product of what you have put into them. We want them to grow up being strong, healthy people. Our tongue has the power of life and death! "The tongue can bring death or life; those who love to talk will reap the consequences." Proverbs 18:21.

"Dear Friends, let us continue to love one another, for love comes from God. Anyone who loves is a child of God and knows God. But anyone who does not love does not know God, for God is love."

"God showed how much He loved us by sending His one and only Son into the world so that we might have eternal life through Him. This is real love - not that we loved God, but that He loved us and sent His Son as a sacrifice to take away our sins."

"Dear friends, since God loved us that much, we surely ought to love each other. No one has ever seen God. But if we love each other, God lives in us, and His love is brought to full expression in us." 1 John 4:7-12.

This is how much God loves us. This is how much Christ loves the church and how much we ought to love each other. This is how much a husband is to love his wife and a wife to love her husband. This is how we ought to see each other, as God living within each other. Our marriage should be the full expression of God in us, the full expression of God's love living within us. We should never take for granted the one God gave to us to cherish and hold till death do us part. Let us cherish.

Many problems start from a person not feeling loved and cherished. Sometimes we can get to a point of judging our spouse, and being judged hurts. "Do not judge others, and you will not be judged. For you will be treated as you treat others. The standard you use in judging is the standard by which you will be judged." Matthew 7:1-2. Remember, you reap what you sow.

"And why worry about the speck in your brother's (interchange husband's or wife's) eye when you have a log in your own? How can you think of saying to your brother (husband/wife), let me help you get rid of that speck in your eye, when you can't see past the log in your own eye? Hypocrite! First get rid of the log in your own eye; then you will see well enough to deal with the speck in your brother's (spouses) eye." I put in "spouse" so that you can look at this scripture in the context of your marriage, as well as of your neighbor.

Let us not judge or be critical of our loved ones. And let's be careful to not take offense to what they are saying to us. If we live with constant judging and criticism, or never being able to please, or feeling offended all the time, there is no happiness in that. This is a breeding ground for the enemy to come and rob, kill and destroy. If we grew up with that, we really need to guard ourselves from acting in that way because we can be doing it and not even realize it. We could be hurting our spouse and not even know it. Forgiving your parents and repenting for judging is the best way to stay free from falling into it. Pray through the process as I have been showing you. **Repent, forgive, break it off your life, in Jesus Name.**

Remember the greatest commandment, Matthew 22:37-39, "Love the Lord your God with all your heart and with all your soul and with all your mind. This is the first and greatest commandment. And the second is like it. Love your neighbor as yourself." Love your family as yourself. I am sure those who have lost family members would say to appreciate them while you have them.

I once knew an elderly person who lost a spouse and grieved deeply, not as much for the loss of the spouse but for how terrible that person had treated the spouse while married. The individual grieved because now they realized how much they did not appreciate the other, and now it was too late. The loved one was gone and the person had failed to love. This elderly person needed to forgive their self; this is a lesson for us to learn. We should treat our spouse as if it were our last day together; and live so we don't regret our actions. We will stand before God for all our words and actions.

The scriptures say, "A man leaves his father and mother and is joined to his wife, and the two are united into one". Eph 5:31. The NKJV says, "the two shall become one flesh." This is a great mystery, but it is an illustration of the way Christ and the church are one. It is just like our relationship with God. When we are born again and spirit-filled, we become ONE with God. When we are married, we become ONE with our spouse. No one can break that. It is a spiritual event. It is a supernatural event. Even divorce does not separate it. Scripture says it can't be done, unless God Himself does it. Maybe this is why it is so painful when people separate, because spiritually they are still bound.

I love the example in the movie, "Fireproof,"[10] of the salt and pepper shakers. When you bind them together and pull them apart, one or both break. That is how it is with marriage, and it is true. I highly recommend watching this film, which shows how to save a dying marriage. It is excellent for those with good marriages.

Individual or Group Questions

1. Together discuss what you need to do better in the area of disciplining. Write a list of new ways of doing it better.

2. In what areas do I need to control my tongue?

3. Name each of your children and spouse/fiancé and list positive attributes of each. Make it a practice to use these positive things to mention and comment to build up your child and spouse/fiancé. Be an encourager.

5. Do We Have Healthy Bonds to Each Other?

It is wrong to unite sexually to another before marriage. God sees more than we do in the spiritual. God's ways are different than our ways. They are much higher. Most do not know the spiritual aspect of sex before marriage. Many are walking around bound to others without marriage. They think that it is over but they are indeed still bound with ungodly soul ties by the act of sexual relations outside of marriage (premarital sex, adultery, and homosexuality). This opens them to demonic influences and curses. This is why God calls us to not do this, for our own protection. People do not get sexual diseases from godly marriage; they are from unmarried partners outside of marriage. Sexual union was designed for married couples to be bound together by the grace of God. If it is done outside of this, it is an open door or gateway for the enemy and outside of God's protective boundaries.

We also remember the example of Jacob and Leah and how they were bound together by marriage by one simple act of a sexual union. Could it be that many are walking around bound to others? How many others? This certainly could affect future relationships, especially our marriage. No wonder so many have daydreams and fantasies about past lovers. The ungodly soul ties need to be broken.

Prayer of Repentance for Sex Outside of Marriage

Pray with your fiancé, spouse, and prayer partner or prayer minister. Unless you both are virgins at the time of marriage, both man and woman must go through these prayers. It's best to have someone agree with you in prayer, but you can pray this alone.

A) Repent for the sin of sex outside of marriage from your heart. Name each person individually, if you can. You can speak these silently to God also. For those whose names you do not know, say "and for those I don't remember."

B) Break all ungodly soul ties with past marriages, past relationships, past engagements, past loves, past sexual unions, and sexual explorations outside of marriage or before marriage, in Jesus' Name. If this applies to you and your spouse having premarital sex, or you and your fiancé, you need repent for this too (and turn from your sin and stop until your wedding night).

Repent for any sexual act that was taking of the other and hurtful to the other, even if you are now married to the person. Forgive the other, if needed. Whether you are married to the person or not, it still opened you up to curses at the time and can affect the marriage bed in a negative way. If this is your spouse or fiancé this will take you being honest because they may have no idea they hurt you. Great healing will take place by doing so. Allow them to repent.

C) Pray to break any curses that came on you from any of these sexual acts, in Jesus' Name. Cancel all the assignments of the enemy that came about from these acts, in Jesus' Name. Cleanse yourself by the Blood of the Lamb. Cleanse all defilement that came onto you and your spouse because of the act(s) of sex outside of marriage. Cleanse them, in Jesus' Name, and call the enemy off of your lives, your marriage bed and from any curse that came onto you. Renounce all ungodly soul ties, connections or bonds with all of the people you have had sexual relations with. Ask God to break

132

all of them off yourself, in Jesus' Mighty Name. Cover both of yourselves and your marriage bed with the Precious Blood of Jesus. Ask the Lord to cleanse and purify you, in Jesus' Name. (These prayers have been proven to make a difference in the sexual lives of marriages.)

D) Have the person praying with you forgive you, in Jesus' Name. If you are alone say, "I accept your forgiveness, Lord." Forgive yourself. Sometimes we are harder on our self and cannot forgive our self. Lord, I forgive myself for this sin. I speak life and blessing into the area of sexual love union in my marriage (or future marriage if you are engaged). Bless my marriage bed Lord. Make it a holy place. Holy Spirit come into my union and fill it with Your Presence. If you are engaged, you need to stop having sex until your wedding night to keep yourselves pure.

E) If rape was experienced, you also, with the above prayer, need to forgive the person who raped you for what he/she did. This will bring great healing. (Remember, it does not mean what the person did was right. This may be difficult to do. Begin forgiving by faith.) Again, break all ungodly soul ties to this person, in Jesus' Name. It is most important to cleanse yourself in the Blood of Jesus. This most likely will need deeper inner healing to take the pain, shame, and false beliefs away. Often there is a false belief that it was your fault. You can pray and ask the Lord Jesus to speak truth to you about the situation to bring light to the dark memory. Renounce all demonic influences, generational spirits that may have come on you at that time, In Jesus' Name, Amen.

A few comments on the Blood of Christ: "Just think how much more the blood of Christ will purify our consciences from sinful deeds so that we can worship the living God." Hebrews 9:14. 1John 1:7 says, "If we walk in the light as He is in the light, we have fellowship with one another, and the Blood of Jesus Christ His Son cleanses us from all sin." Romans 3:23 says, "All have sinned." Sin results in spiritual uncleanness. Water and many other solvents are used to wash away physical uncleanness, but only the Blood of Christ can cleanse us from sin.

Also, often rape is a generational curse. You may find that your mother and grandmother or aunts were raped as well. If you don't have knowledge of it, you can still pray to break the generational curse of rape off your life and the lives of your children, future grand children, and future generations to the end of time, in Jesus Name. Follow the breaking of generational curses prayer for this.

F) RAPE - If you did the rape or any type of force or molesting, the use of pornography and any sexual sin, then you need to have a deep repentance, sincerely from your heart, in Jesus' Name. Have someone forgive you. Or say, "I receive the Lord's forgiveness." You probably need to forgive yourself as well. You may very well need a generational curse broken off your life and/or need more extensive prayer. Go back to the prayer of breaking that generational curse off your life. All sexual sin needs the spirit of lust to be broken off your lives, in Jesus Name. Repent for letting the Spirit of lust in your life. Repent for the Spirit of control.

You also will need to forgive whoever did similar things to you, and break off that which came on you. Name each person you did this with, and repent from your heart. It is best to have

someone praying over you for Deliverance while you agree with them in prayer. You must have someone who is living a righteous life and anointed with the Holy Spirit. Sample prayer, "I loose from myself the Spirit of lust and control, right now, from my life in Jesus' Name, and any other demons I opened myself up to. List as the Spirit reveals. I command them to leave me and my life right now, in Jesus' Mighty Name. Amen."

G) If there are any children out of wedlock, pray that all curses that came upon them be broken, in Jesus' Name. Ask the Lord to break it off. Cancel the assignment of the enemy off your children and cleanse them by the Blood of the Lamb, Jesus. Dedicate your children to the Lord. Call down the generational blessings and spiritual gifts upon them, in the Mighty Name of Jesus.

Individual or Group Questions

1. How did you do during the week encouraging people and speaking only positive?

2. Where could you do better? Try it again this week.

3. Pray and repent for being negative. Ask the Lord for help in doing this and starting a habit in your life to be an encourager and person who brings life to people. Accept His forgiveness.

6. *Fruit of the Spirit in Marriage*

"But the fruit of the Spirit is love, joy, peace, patience, kindness, goodness, faithfulness, gentleness and self-control." Galatians 5:22. As Christians, we should be walking in these attributes. We are not perfect and we will fail our wife or husband. But home is where we need to *practice* these, and they will flow from us as we walk out our daily life with other people. We are an example, so these attributes will rub off on our children, and they will walk that way too. Even if they stray, they will come back to the way they have been trained up. "Direct your children onto the right path and when they are older they will not leave it." Proverb 22:6.

"Let the Holy Spirit guide your lives. Then you won't be doing what your sinful nature craves. The sinful nature wants to do evil, which is the opposite of what the Spirit wants. And the Spirit gives us desires that are the opposite of what the sinful nature desires. These two forces are constantly fighting each other, so you are not free to carry out your good intentions." NIV Galatians 5:16.

Just reading the scriptures is not enough; we must live by the scriptures, and this will help us to have a good marriage. Galatians 5:17 says that these two natures are continuously fighting each other. This is why being equally yoked--equally bound--to another who has the same spirit helps a lot for a happy marriage. I've seen many people struggle in marriages that were unequally yoked.

"When you follow the desires of your sinful nature, the results are very clear: sexual immorality, impurity, lustful pleasures, idolatry, sorcery, hostility, quarreling, jealousy, outbursts of anger, selfish ambition, dissension, division, envy, drunkenness, wild parties, and other sins like these. Let me tell you again, as I have before, that anyone living that sort of life will not inherit the Kingdom of God." Galatians 5:19.

"Those who belong to Christ Jesus have nailed the passions and desires of their sinful nature to His cross and crucified them there. Since we are living by the Spirit, let us follow the Spirit's leading in every part of our lives. Let us not become conceited or provoke one another or be jealous of one another." Galatians 5:24.

This is difficult at times, but we must keep the fruits of the Spirit alive within us. The best way to keep the Holy Spirit alive within us is to stay close to our Lord.

If we find we have more negative fruit rather than the positive fruit of the Spirit, then we are backsliding. Often this can happen so gradually that we don't even realize. We must stay in the Word and stay connected to a Spirit-filled church and others spiritually equal to us; most of all stay connected to God.

If we have been set free, let us stay free and not get caught up in the sins of the world. Separate yourself from that way of life, and from those who live that way, if it is going to cause you to sin. We become like those we hang around; be careful of co-workers, friends, and even family. If they are not living right, it can steer us in the wrong direction and cause us to sin. Normally it is uncomfortable to be around those who live like this. Slowly, we can backslide and the enemy tells us it is ok. We can begin to compromise when the enemy says, "It's ok! It won't hurt to do this. Everyone is doing it." Often we can pick up a demon or two by hanging around the wrong places and also by sinning. Our mind can get transformed into a mind of the world.

We should be growing in the strength of the Lord to eventually be able to withstand being around the influence of people of the world, to be a good influence and be a witness to the Glory of God in our lives. Jesus did this. But we must be prayed up and strong for this, living a higher level in the Holy Spirit. But if it is a temptation to be around those who live worldly lives, then we must separate ourselves from them. If we are still hanging out in bars and getting drunk, we are backsliding big time. If you don't see it then you are being deceived by the enemy.

We are to be kind hearted to one another and be peacemakers, forgiving one another; this begins in our home. We are to let God rule in our hearts, home, family, and marriage. This brings a Holy Spirit environment for us and our children to grow in. It gives them an example of what their home should be when they grow up. It sets a standard, a foundation for them to build their futures on so as to soar even higher in the Lord than we have. They will treat their husbands, wives, and children with great love and respect if that is what they have seen in their home.

"Always be humble and gentle. Be patient with each other, making allowance for each other's faults because of your love. Make every effort to keep yourselves united in the Spirit, binding yourselves together with peace." Ephesians 4:2.

"Understand this, my dear brothers and sisters: You must be quick to listen, slow to speak, and slow to get angry. Human anger does not produce the righteousness God desires. So get rid of all the filth and evil in your lives, and humbly accept the word God has planted in your hearts, for it has the power to save your souls. But don't just listen to God's word. You must do what it says. Otherwise, you are only fooling yourselves." James 1:19-22.

There will be times when we fall. There will be times of disagreement in our marriage and family. We must use the scriptures and fruits of the Spirit as a guide of how to act, using self-control and keeping our eyes on God, being loving and kind. If we fall, we must forgive ourselves, stand up and brush ourselves off and keep going.

Individual or Group Questions

1. List the 9 Fruits of the Spirit. (Gal. 5:22)

2. Look up in the Bible Philippians 4:8. List godly attributes.

3. Look up 1 Corinthians 3:12. List 6 things we are to wear or "put on".

4. Look up 1 Corinthians 3:13 4-8. List godly attributes.

7. Honor & Respect

It can become a habit and way of life to treat our spouses in a disrespectful way. If we've been married for a long time most likely we have done it for so long we have absolutely no idea that we have been disrespectful. The more disrespectful we are, the more our marital problems grow. We are sowing bad seeds into the marriage and into the other person. We can't expect goodness out of a person that we have been treating badly.

We must celebrate each other's individuality; it is for this reason that we were first attracted to them. There is no other person on earth like him/her. The same is true for our children; we must respect and love them as children of God and celebrate who they are, each unique in their own way. When we do this, they will learn to respect and be tolerant of others too. There is no one else in the world like your spouse. God chose that person for you. He/she is so special. Always be mindful of what drew you to the other to begin with…what made you fall in love with that person. Celebrate the uniqueness and the gifts which make your loved one who he or she is…the one you fell in love with. If each is doing this for the other, nobody is starved for attention or individuality. If our individuality is not allowed to be free, it can lead to problems; in time it can lead to an identity crisis. This doesn't have to be. We should be thriving in who we are in our marriage, not squashed or controlled or over-run by the other. It is a mutual walk in the Lord. No one should be lost in the marriage, but both should continue to grow and thrive as individual people.

The walk of marriage should be like someone joining us in the journey towards God; both of us are on the same team, and best friends; both of us are running the race, loving God with all our hearts, souls and strength. Our journey to the Lord does not have to be one in which we hurt the one we love.

Often life gets difficult, but if we focus on the Lord rather than the problem it is easier to get through. Again, as I said earlier, if we focus on the negative it seems much worse than it really is. Often when we focus on the Lord we can rise above the situation in our life. Often we begin to see the problem through His eyes and that is where there is a good solution. He helps us get through.

John Sandford says, "We are designed to grind," meaning that God brings us together to grind each other into a more perfect vessel for God. This is often painful. Growing can be painful but the outcome is wonderful. If we respect and honor one another and look out for each other, we can continue to be close. It's when we are out for number one and we become self-centered that trouble starts.

Some feel that they are the boss, the one who gets his/her own way and that the spouse has no opinion. Let us remember that this is our spouse's only life, a life that is so precious and created by God. We can make it or break it. Our spouses need the freedom to spread their wings and fly, to grow and be at peace, because this is the only life they have on earth...with us. You don't want it to be a jail sentence, which is how I hear some people describe their many years of marriage. No, it should not be a jail sentence; it should be FREEDOM! It should be freedom to be who we are...free to grow and love life to the fullest, and to grow in the Lord and serve Him.

I feel the Lord urging me to share more about honor. We see in the scriptures that it will go well with us and we will have long life, if we honor our parents.

There really seems to be no honor these days. I was heartbroken at the dishonor that a Christian President, President Bush, got when he was in office by not only the world but also by the body of Christ. I was absolutely shocked at the mean and vile things that were said about him by Christians in editorials, tearing him apart so viciously that I was ashamed to call myself a Christian. What kind of Body are we? It is evil to tear each other apart. That should not be! Why aren't we praying for our president? What kind of country are we? A country divided cannot stand; the enemy is counting on this. I was very worried about the condition of the Body of Christ. I had no idea that Christians were so hateful. If we cannot honor a Christian President, then how can we honor in our homes?

In homes husbands are not honoring their wives, wives are not honoring their husbands, children are not honoring their parents and parents are not honoring their children. Where does it end? It is a ripple effect in our society. When we honor a human being, we honor God. When we honor our leader, we honor God. It doesn't mean we have to agree with that person. When we honor, we treat another as valuable and precious. When we honor, we value one another. Society trains us to dishonor. We are a very judging nation. Often when I am in intercession for our country, God has me repent for the judging done by Christians. It seems to be in our culture and it needs to stop. We are not part of this world. I am shocked at those on television and how harsh they are at degrading one another in reality shows, talk shows and in the media. I am shocked and appalled. As Christians, we cannot join in with this.

"Cursed is the man who dishonors his father and mother." Deuteronomy 27:16. Do we know this today? Does our society know this? How quickly we can curse ourselves. Do we know it in our marriage? I don't think so. When we honor each other, it teaches our children to honor not only parents but also their teachers, bosses, the law and authority figures. It teaches us to not be rebellious.

David honored Saul in spite of Saul having tried to kill him and doing evil. This shows us that we should honor them not because what they do is right, but because God put them in authority. In John 19:10, Pilate said, "Don't you realize that I have the power to release you or crucify you?" Then Jesus said, "You would have no power over me at all unless it was given to you from above." Jesus is saying that all power and authority comes from God and God appoints them. That means if you do not like our president, realize though that God has a purpose and you should not work against it. God has a purpose. By honoring them, we honor God and His plans.

Many are upset about President Obama getting into office since he stands for many unrighteous things. I am not happy, but with all the prayer and fasting that went out for God's will to be done, I have to agree, this must be the man God allowed. The reason for this, we do not fully know, but God is in charge and He is not taken by surprise. God is in control in order to fulfill the word of the Lord. Paul said in Acts 23:5, "Do not speak evil against your ruler." Many of us need to repent for this, me included. It is ok to be aware of the evil being done so that we can pray for justice and God's will. We need to be praying for our president, congress, and all those in governmental leadership positions.

143

Many are looking for revival in our land and it begins with us repenting, loving and honoring. "Then if My people who are called by My Name will humble themselves and pray and seek My face and turn from their wicked ways, I will hear from heaven and will forgive their sins and restore their land." 2 Chronicles 7:14 People, right now our land needs restoring! We need to get right with God. It begins in our hearts and in our homes.

Individual or Group Questions

1. In what ways have I "not" honored and respected my spouse/fiancé and children where I judge or am critical of them?

2. In what ways can I honor and respect my spouse/fiancé more?

3. List the very things that caused you fall in love with your spouse/fiancé.

8. Listen

Be watchful and protective of each other in your marriage. Does the other one need help? Just because it is one's job to do something doesn't mean he or she is not overloaded or behind and in need of a helping hand. Maybe they are always behind and seem to always need help or more time. Listen and watch for hints of the needs of your loved one: physical, sexual, or spiritual, spoken and unspoken words. Care! Often times one can speak his/her need but not be heard or cared about. Sometimes we get tunnel vision, looking only to ourselves, and we become deaf to the needs of our spouse or family. This is for those married for many years or only a few. We learn to have to look out for ourselves because nobody else will if we don't. We can become hard and callused to the needs of our spouse. This can only get worse as time goes on. Often it is good when trouble arises, because these issues can surface and come to a head and be dealt with. That is why a marriage gets stronger as time goes on; many issues having been dealt with are conquered.

No one knows your spouse better than you. At least that should be so. You can see signs of whatever your spouse needs, so be sensitive to those needs. Stay attuned to your husband's or wife's likes and dislikes.

For the first time, I participated in a Secret Sister program at church. You find out things about a sister in church and secretly you pray for that person and her prayer needs. You do random acts of kindness for your Secret Sister. You buy her little things that you know she would like and send her cards, candy, flowers, etc. As I began doing this, I realized that this is what we should be doing for our spouses. God showed me that we should be getting to know everything about them...their likes and dislikes. We should be doing random acts of kindness for them, picking up maybe their favorite desert, candy, flowers, and sending love notes or cards. Men like random acts of kindness, flowers, plants, books, tools and surprises too. It might be something to enhance your spouse's hobbies; you might buy the other a shirt or just do little things for your spouse or leave little notes, hold doors open for the other. Maybe it could be a surprise night out to a movie or you could go on a picnic; be creative with random acts of kindness.

These kinds of things spark the flame of romance that, after many years, can tend to grow dim or even blow out. Then you look and say, hey! Where is the romance? This is boring. I don't even know if I am in love any longer. Well what have you put into the marriage? Could be the last five to ten years you were taking your spouse for granted? This definitely should not be happening with newlyweds, but I've seen it. Be aware, because it happens when we get so used to each other and we take each other for granted. Or perhaps we are so used to being alone that when we marry, we live the single life in our marriage by blocking the other out.

Dating should never end after we get married. Never stop dating your spouse and especially not after children; it is in these years you need it the most. How about a surprise night out to dinner or movie; yes, you women too, nothing is just for men or just for women. You could go for a walk, a drive, hiking, picnic, tennis, or some sport, or out for ice cream. Take a class together or share in making some type of craft. Make their favorite dinner, snack, or dessert. Many women cook night after night; what a delight it would be to have someone say...you sit down and I will make dinner tonight for you. Or if the husband does all the cooking, then gals give them a break, maybe once a week; be creative. Is the house pretty messy? Does your spouse need a helping hand? Help without getting angry. Or a helping hand with the kids? How about a vacation, do some traveling. The ideas can be endless and creative; candlelight dinner and/or soft worship music in the bedroom. Did you ever fix your spouse breakfast in bed? How about a massage? Let us never stop treating our spouse special, like we treated them in the beginning. Many need to repent for this. Some not only take them for granted but many treat their spouses down right bad. Instead of being sarcastic and cold, we can be loving and sensitive.

We must have a date night. Can't afford to? Budget it in as you would a bill, to go out once a week or twice a month to dinner, a movie, for a walk, hiking, boating, tennis, or camping. We do this! Every Friday is date night and we look forward to it. Take an annual vacation or short weekend getaway---go here and there---be creative. Go away to a Christian Conference. We always planned our vacations around revivals. Go on a mission trip. Don't get in a rut. Enjoy each other and enjoy the world God created by seeing the handiwork of His hands. Life has to go beyond your home or you'll soon get in a rut and depression can set in. Sometimes life can get hard, and we get tossed by the wind of the storms, but we have each other. We need each other. Don't distance yourself from the one you love; stand together. Stand together with the Lord; three cords are not easily broken. Get involved in a ministry, mission trip, or volunteer your time to help for example a soup kitchen. This keeps us working for God and to enjoy a fulfilling life. We are happiest when we fill our lives with God.

There are many possibilities such as getting out, having friends, and laughing and enjoying life that help keep life positive. We start out with just the two of us when we marry; kids come, they grow up and they go and we return to just the two of us again. So set your foundation right. You're a team---best friends---that does not end, till death do us part. Do some of these things to put love back into your relationship. Do it without the kids. Often we can let the children get between us. Take time to nourish your relationship. A fire will soon go out if we do not put logs on it. What have you done lately to keep the flames of your love and passion for each other?

Individual or Group Questions

1. Discuss and list things you can do to get out together and have fun. Listen to each others suggestions and make a list together.

2. In what areas do I need more of a helping hand from my spouse/fiancé? Discuss lovingly.

3. List things you can lovingly do for your spouse in loving surprises.

9. *Friends*

Friends can bring freshness into our relationships. Friends are a gift from God, laughs and fun. Too often, as time goes on in a marriage and babies come, the kids grow and responsibilities grow; people lose their smiles and sense of humor. It is sad but too often true. We can get buried in the burdens of life.

The Scriptures say we are to be childlike. This takes different forms. Children not only are obedient, trusting and dependent on their parents, but children play and surely know how to have fun. Children are open to new things and are creative. Let us not have all work and no play. That would be unhealthy and unbalanced for a child and for an adult as well. Having busy lives but not having time for each other, or no fun together, is not right. How enjoyable is marriage then? We used to laugh a lot before marriage, fool around and goof off, and that should never change. We must take time for laughs and joy.

I used to be one who took life too seriously. For a season I rarely smiled. Sometimes life gets hard and you get into bad habits. Hard times can steal the joy of life away and you forget to smile; it should not be that way. The enemy works to steal your joy and uses your children at times. We can have joy in the midst of trials. Praise the Lord during your trials, pray in tongues, and put your trust in Him. Don't take life too seriously. Don't let life get you down so much that you do not enjoy life. If we get too serious we will be hard and cold as we grow older. We've all seen people like that. Is that how we want to be? Really, this is where the enemy would steal our joy. What good are we for the Lord if we are hard and cold?

God is the same yesterday, today and tomorrow, but we must grow to change, to reach and understand more of Him and to be more like Him. What kind of parents would we be if we were always hard and cold? Yet many of us can be this way. What kind of Christians would we be? Who would want to become a Christian or have what we have if we are cold and hard hearted. That does not reflect God at all. If you find yourself being this way, pray with your spouse or strong Christian friend or those at your church. This will free you up. Using some of the prayers in this book can help to release joy in your life when you call the enemy off your life.

Let us be sure to not only have fun and joke with friends and co-workers, but let's save some fun and laughter for our marriage and family too. We must never outgrow this. Laughter is healthy for our bodies. This means the opposite, bitterness, is bad for our bodies.

"A cheerful heart is good medicine. But a crushed spirit dries up the bones." NIV Proverb 17:22. Ezekiel chapter 37 shows us that dried bones have no life, no spirit of God. It can even mean old. Even scientific studies have shown that laughter is good for the body and soul. In the recent revivals, God gave holy laughter to set people free. People were actually delivered from years of deep depression while blessed with holy laughter. God is so good. Only with God can we laugh our way to wholeness.

My husband is funny and used to joke with everyone at work. I rarely saw that part of him at home for a season; he seemed so serious. Most likely it was because I did not laugh at his jokes and did not appreciate that quality in him. I was too busy in life to find anything funny. Could also be things were just too serious at home and we did not joke at home.

Then I got hit by the Holy Spirit through Revival in the 90s, and God gave me holy laughter and I began to laugh again. I lightened up! I was born again and Spirit-filled but had lost my joy. God released joy on me. Sometimes I would laugh so hard I thought I would die but in that, God delivered me of some things.

I feel young again and can laugh and can have fun. If you were to ask my husband, he would tell you that I was not like that before we were married. When we dated we laughed and played games and had lots of fun; somewhere in all the responsibilities of parenting and adult responsibilities that got lost. Somehow the enemy stole my joy. I grew up too much. Being grown up does not mean being too serious and it does not mean we don't laugh anymore; yes, we need to be responsible but don't let trials steal your joy. We are to be childlike and the Holy Spirit keeps us young and our marriage alive and fresh. It is hard when there are big trials. Pray in tongues and praise the Lord.

"Always be full of joy in the Lord. I say it again - rejoice! Let everyone see that you are considerate in all you do. Remember, the Lord is coming soon. Don't worry about anything; instead, pray about everything. Tell God what you need and thank Him for all he has done. Then you will experience God's peace, which exceeds anything we can understand. His peace will guard your hearts and minds as you live in Christ." Philippians 4:4.

What a great recipe to joy and peace. If you find your husband or wife is not joyful or not having fun anymore, you must look at yourself and see if you have sown some unhealthy seeds in your marriage. Maybe we are miserable acting. Women, this can happen when we have hormonal problems, get deep in the cares of parenting, financial problems, or life in general.

"The joy of the Lord is my strength." There is actually strength in joy and laughter. It will help you get through life easier; I know, I've been there. The Psalms say, "He pours oil of joy on us. "The joy of the Lord is my strength!" Nehemiah 8:10. Ask for it if you need it and you will receive joy. So that is what Holy Laughter is, God pouring oil of joy upon us.

"And the believers were filled with joy and with the Holy Spirit." Acts 13:52. Joy comes with the Holy Spirit. What does that look like? What does it look like when God pours oil of joy upon us and people are being baptized in the Holy Spirit and with JOY? It probably looks like a lot of laughing. Joy and laughter do not automatically come together with being baptized with the Holy Spirit. The Bible lists Joy and the Holy Spirit as separate. They don't necessarily have to come together, but they can. Guard your joy. Now that I have my joy back, I would never want to lose it. Life is happier and so is my marriage. I actually feel younger with joy. I do have to stand guard because I did lose it again partially. I saw how it went too. Worry, trials with our teens, attacks of the enemy. Keep watch.

I am afraid many people can lose their sense of humor along the pathway of life. We have a wonderful family. When we all get together, we laugh a lot and hard; people were commenting on all the laughter. I said laughter is healthy for our bodies. One woman was surprised and said to me, "Really, I haven't laughed in years." I felt so bad for her and for her spouse. We can be sure stress will come, so we must be sure we have joy in our lives and not get buried alive, depressed and oppressed with the troubles in our lives. I truly believe staying close to God keeps the heart light and youthful. If you've lost your joy or maybe never had it, ask God for it and draw unto Him.

"He will once again fill your mouth with laughter and your lips with shouts of joy." Job 8:21. Make this a prayer...Lord; once again fill my mouth with laughter and joy.

"We were filled with laughter, and we sang for joy." Psalm 126:2. Joyful songs and praise songs bring joy to the heart. Draw close to God and the Holy Spirit will release joy.

"Come to me, all of you who are weary and carry heavy burdens, and I will give you rest. Take up My yoke upon you. Let me teach you, because I am humble and gentle at heart, and you will find rest for your souls. For my yoke is easy to bear, and the burden I give you is light." Matthew 11:28.

Friends are a way we can have fun; girlfriends for the women, guy friends for the guys. Couple friends are very important for us as a couple as well. I remember years when we had no friends, and we prayed and begged God for good and godly couples. It was needed; people of the same values. Let us always remember that our spouses are our best friends in the whole world. Others will come and go but our spouses are our life mates. They should be our best friends. It becomes off balance when we begin to share everything with someone other than our husband or wife. Yes, of course it is good to share and have friends, but we need to be careful when someone else takes their place; it can become spiritual adultery. Our husband or wife can be shoved aside when this happens. This can happen with a child, when we share and become so close with our son or daughter, and they somehow take the place or push the spouse away. This leaves the other spouse left out with the feeling of abandonment and loneliness. Make sure you have a healthy relationship with your parents and your children and are not leaving your husband or wife out.

When we share our heart with another, then we lack communication with our own spouse; it can hurt our relationship. Actually friends should complement our marriage, never take away from it. If that isn't happening, then something is not right and it should be examined.

Beware of getting too close to someone of the opposite sex, where the enemy can get in and cause trouble, even if they are Christian. When we start with the level of sharing and communicating too much with the opposite sex, which is where a relationship of the wrong kind can begin to replace what we have with our spouse.

Of course there is the ability to be friends with the opposite sex with no problems and just have brotherly or sisterly love. But, guard yourselves, because the enemy can run with it. Make sure it does not pass over to a danger zone. When we begin sharing and enjoying other persons more than our spouses, we must cut it off. This is where trouble begins with one falling in love with another. It begins with intimate communication. Or one taking the place of, or filling in, where our spouses or marriages are lacking.

Sometimes friends of the same sex can be needy and drain us. Some people are unhealthy for us to be too close to; they suck up our good energy and rely too much upon us. Friends, or even relatives, can be this way. Be aware if this is happening, and you can back off lovingly.

Through the years we will make many healthy, godly, wonderful friendships. Many come and many go, crossing paths for a short time, according to the plan of the Lord. Many are divine connections who we need to meet for our call and destiny and God's purposes in our lives, and in their lives as well. Enjoy people because they are God's creation and gift to you.

In a marriage, it is good for you both to have interests, and best if done together, but it is healthy to have your own hobbies, interests, likes and dislikes too. It is healthy to be separate at times, but be aware of continuously leaving one alone too much; a sense of loneliness and even abandonment can set in his or her heart. If one is left too much and too soon in the marriage, a depression can set in that one's heart. We cannot neglect our beloved husband or beloved wife; they are so precious. They should feel loved and needed. If you have many interests that are not the same, make sure you both have some interests that are the same too; focus on them as well.

When your loved one shares his or her experiences, listen, really care, and really hear the person. Beware of neglecting your spouse. This is how the fire goes out and resentment can set in. The temptation of searching for new, greener pastures can come.

Simple things make a difference, such as, if when you are together one of you is always on the computer, or always sleeping, always having your face in the television, always reading or always pursuing a hobby, it can make the other feel shut out. You must make sure you have quality time together to make a marriage work. Often times it may take a conscious effort to include the other. On the other hand accept that your loved one has gifts, talents, and hobbies, don't be jealous of them.

For many people, quality time together is their identification of love. Before marriage you spent quality time together, so why not afterwards? Why would that change? It is equally important after you're married to continue to have a healthy marriage. Again, life and jobs can get in the way but work around it and make time for each other when you can.

Having your alone time and own interests is important, but just be aware of blocking others in your home out. This goes for blocking the children out as well; they, too, need quality time. It gets more difficult juggling responsibilities. Again that word, balance; we are body, soul and spirit, and we need to live balanced lives to have each part of us be healthy and nourished. We need to eat right, exercise our bodies and spirits to be healthy, complete people. Don't let yourself go; keep yourself the best you can be in every way for God, and look and be your best for yourself as well as for your spouse. When you care about how you look, it communicates that you care about yourself and your spouse. Just because you got your spouse, is no reason to let yourself go. Be clean, groomed, and dress decent. Sometimes we can see ourselves as slobs and only look good when you go out. No, look nice for each other. It will make you feel good about yourself.

Be very careful who you spend a lot of time with, whether family or friends; they must have the same standards as your family. Certainly everyone is different and everyone's standards differ. "Bad company corrupts good morals." 1 Corinthians 15:33. Friends are a gift from God.

Individual or Group Questions

1. In what ways can I lighten up more and laugh more?

2. In what ways can I bring joy into my home?

3. What things are stealing our joy in our life?

4. Discuss remedies with spouse/fiancé.

5. Is there something lacking from our marriage? What?

10. Compromise

Sometimes this word is looked upon as not good. We should never compromise our walk with the Lord. We should not compromise morality. We should not compromise our spirituality, but sometimes we're forced to when we are unequally yoked, and this is very painful for those who experience it. Even though both may be born again Christians, we grow differently. One may be more open to the Lord or freer in the Holy Spirit than the other. One may grow more rapidly and we may feel an unequal-ness, even in a Christian marriage. Our beloved may not be where we are at, and we can't force them to grow or slow down; we must wait for God to give revelation on a number of things. We can gently love and guide each other. Be an example, but ultimately it is up to the Lord to bring the other one through. I have heard women talk about their husbands not being spiritually mature; then I spent time talking with the husband and heard deep spiritual wisdom. Don't expect your spouse to be a carbon copy of you. It may not look just like you but yet be maturity. Different gifts and different callings look different.

Many were married first before coming to the Lord, and then only one of you came into the fullness of the Lord. You must love and gently speak God's truth here and there, when God makes a way, but ultimately it is God who gives the power to change through the Holy Spirit. We do not need to shove God down the other one's throat. This also goes for our grown children. Many of us have made this mistake. This comes from feeling like we are the ones who need to save our spouses, or grown children. It is not in our control to save a person; it is a free gift from God, and we can only gently plant seeds and water them. This is where patience is very important as well as gentleness.

Scripture says to love them to the Lord. Living the gospel will speak louder than words ever will; it will do more to bring them in than pushing, preaching, judging or condemning them. Just think of all the seeds scattered throughout your home by merely loving and living the word. We need to repent for judging and condemning because it makes them put walls up against us and the Lord. We may even need to go directly to them to apologize and hug them. Then start new by loving!

"Most important of all, continue to show deep love for each other, for love covers a multitude of sins." 1 Peter 4:8. How much more we are to show deep love for each other in our homes. Maybe we were not brought up that way, but we can overcome that by doing what is right. It will be easier to overcome when we forgive our parents and break free from those judgments we've sown.

"Wives, in the same way be submissive to your husbands so that, if any of them does not believe the word, they may be won over without words by the behavior of their wives, when they see the purity and reverence of your lives." NIV 1 Peter 3:1.

You may have to do this with family members; loving, without pushing. Living the gospel speaks louder than words. If you are unequally yoked in a relationship but not married yet, you better have heard from the Lord that he or she is the right one for you, because it can be difficult. "Do not be yoked together with unbelievers. For what do righteousness and wickedness have in common? Or what fellowship can light have with darkness?" NIV 2 Corinthians 6:14.

Know that you know you are choosing the right mate. Don't just follow your heart but follow God. We know of someone whose husband was saved by the Lord at their own wedding. So know that you know God has called you to this person for life.

"If a Christian man has a wife who is not a believer and she is willing to continue living with him, he must not leave her. And if a Christian woman has a husband who is not a believer and he is willing to continue living with her, she must not leave him. For the Christian wife brings holiness to her marriage, and the Christian husband brings holiness to his marriage. Otherwise your children would not be holy but now they are holy." 1 Corinthians 7:12.

Basically this is saying that divorce defiles the child. This is sad, because so many children today are from broken marriages. It affects the children and their hearts. We need to pray over children from broken marriages and ask God to cover them with the Precious Blood of Jesus and to cleanse them and make them whole again.

In a marriage relationship we both have ideas, wants, and needs, and we must at times compromise ours to bless the other in fairness. Never should one "always" get his or her way. This would cause one to feel powerless, stifled and unfulfilled. Men and women both have wisdom for the direction for the family. Both of us have the potential of hearing wrongly. If one is very much against something, you better listen, care, and not be headstrong. Don't compromise morality or your relationship with the Lord, of course, but both sides may have to compromise in different ways.

Compromising is doing some things that we really don't want to, for the sake of our beloved ones. Maybe, I like to always do something one way and my husband likes to do it another way. We can compromise, by sometimes doing it our way and sometimes doing things their way. Often it comes down to a guy's way or a girl's way. In some marriages, that may never be an issue but in others it will.

Some say a marriage should be 50/50; this may mean you give half and I give half, but we must put into the marriage 100%/100%. We should put our entire effort into it, our best. Both should be allowed to be their whole self, not compromising who they are but being accepted for who they are. This can be hard if you yourself were not accepted for who you were when you were growing up. You may not know how to accept your spouse for who he/she is. This can be caused by our parents not accepting us for who we were or controlling us. We must forgive our parent(s) for this; maybe it still is ongoing. We must continue to forgive and also break those ungodly soul ties that cause them to have ungodly power over us. I have seen middle-aged men and women not having freedom to make good choices in their lives because of fear that their parents wouldn't like it.

Having a healthy relationship with our parents and in-laws is wonderful, but we may have to back off a bit if there are control issues. It may take sitting down and telling them gently and lovingly, yet firmly, that we are grown now with our own family and can make our own decisions. We must take it to God; He will direct our path. If there is a healthy relationship with our parents, we are open to wanting their advice. It is good to get the wisdom or help from our elders when needed. We can learn from their experiences. I have found that simple prayers of breaking ungodly ties work miraculously.

Our marriage should be important to us because it is our life. After a while, it will not be foremost on our mind because we will learn to walk in it without thinking about it. That is why it is good to look at things written in this book, because we may be doing all right or we may be going in the wrong direction, heading for a crash, without realizing it. We always must CARE! If one is unhappy, the other should care. It is a cop out to not care, compromise and stretch yourself.

There will be times when our love will transition from that early, madly in love with each other feeling, to a consistent steadfast love, loving and accepting each other for who we are. Sometimes love is a choice. There is no reason why your relationship can't stay fresh by just loving on each other and blessing each other. Again, our marriage is our life, and if we are happy in our marriage, we'll be happier in all other areas of our life.

Just like in our marriage, we can lose that passion with the Lord that we had in the beginning, like losing our first love. We need to keep our relationship alive, fresh and passionate with God. If we put our relationship on the back burner and take it for granted, it will fizzle away. The world will take over and so will the enemy. If you neglect a garden, weeds pop up, take over, and choke out good fruit. With a little care and effort, we could have large healthy fruits and vegetables instead of small, unhealthy, worm and bug infested fruits and vegetables. The same will happen to our marriage if it is meaningless to us or ignored.

Let's keep our marriage fresh by both running hard after God together, making Him the center of our lives and marriage. Putting God first and our spouse second, this makes for a very healthy marriage. What helped us at a critical time was reading the scriptures together. This not only strengthened our marriage but brought salvation to our hearts. Start with the Gospel of

John. Take turns reading to each other nightly before bedtime.

Sometimes one has to be strong while the other is weak, and vice-versa. A single person does not have this advantage; they follow the Lord alone. There are times when I feel weak, and my husband has just the right words and strength to help me along. Other times I am strong when he is feeling down and out; God designed us to help each other.

From the beginning, I learned we should be working for God, being His hands and feet in the world. This is very rewarding when done together and is very good for a marriage. Try to get trained together, and certainly serve the Lord together if possible. It is very powerful to work for God together as a husband and wife team. It is very rewarding. Sometimes jobs don't allow this but go to church on Sundays, to prayer meetings, revival meetings, conferences, and bible studies together. Stay filled with the Holy Spirit together, keep learning and growing in the Lord to keep yourselves equally yoked spiritually.

We are two different individuals, with individual needs to our personalities and body makeup. For example, my husband loves to give massages. Oh, how I love that trait. All my kids inherited the talent to give good massages at a young age. They just seemed to have been born knowing how to give a great massage. I don't, and I never liked giving massages. Is that fair? No. So I must compromise, stretch myself and give some massages, too, or I won't be getting any!

Maybe one hates to do dishes, so the other helps out to assist the other. Maybe one likes one kind of music; the other likes another...this can be difficult.

Country music to me is like nails on a chalk board, but my husband loves it. This was difficult for me years ago when he started really getting into listening to it. It REALLY bothered me a lot. I didn't think I'd make it through. I was convinced we were not right for each other. Fortunately it is not the only type of music he likes. He got so that he would only listen to it in his workshop in the basement when he was away from me. He compromised! I can't tell you how much this helped our marriage. Something as simple as that shook my world. There are ways to have a happy marriage when we have our differences by compromising, being considerate, and trying to understand and respect each others differences. This certainly is the case with cultural, religious and nationality differences.

Individual or Group Questions

1. Do I want things my way all the time?

2. In what ways do I need to compromise more?

3. On a scale of 1-10 how passionate am I toward my spouse/fiancé? (Ten being very passionate.)

4. On a scale of 1-10 how passionate is my spouse/fiancé towards me?

5. Share and discuss your answers.

11. Sexual Compatibility

Sex, also, is a gift from God that only goes with marriage. Many try to sneak and use that gift before it's time. The enemy has perverted God's gift which is easy for him to do since many use this gift outside of God's protective boundary, which is marriage. This will have an adverse affect on us when we marry.

Marital Sex can be a wonderful experience, or the most frustrating in different ways. Many married couples are fully compatible sexually and many are not. Maybe both want to be in union a lot, or maybe both want very little. That is not the case for all married couples. When one has a higher sexual drive and the other has a low sexual drive or none, then that is another time where compromise comes in on both sides to close the gap.

Some may have been abused and are afraid of sex or even despise sex, because they have not experienced the holiness of it but only what the devil has inflicted upon them. This can make for a very unhappy portion of the marriage. Maybe the marriage is strong in every other way, but sexually there is imbalance. This can eventually affect other parts of the relationship. Remember to compromise, and be loving, patient, and gentle with each other. You must remember that you cannot cut one off sexually, because you risk pushing the other into sin. If though there is a reason you cannot like infidelity and you feel you are at risk of disease, then get yourselves tested.

"Each man should have his own wife and each woman should have her own husband. The husband should fulfill his wife's sexual needs and the wife should fulfill her husband's needs. The wife gives authority over her body to her husband and the husband gives authority over his body to his wife." 1 Corinthians 7:3, 4.

"Do not deprive each other of sexual relations unless you both agree to refrain from sexual intimacy for a limited time so you can give yourselves more completely to prayer. Afterward, you should come together again so that satan won't be able to tempt you because of your lack of self-control. I say this as a concession not as a command. But I wish everyone were single just as I am. But God gives to some the gift of marriage and to others the gift of singleness." 1 Corinthians 7:5.

"But for those who are married, I have a command that comes not from me, but from the Lord. A wife must not leave her husband. But if she does leave him, let her remain single or else be reconciled to him. And the husband must not leave his wife." 1 Corinthians 7:10.

Many marriages are at risk of adultery when one cuts the other off from a sexual relationship; also it may push the man into pornography. This, too, is harmful to the marriage and a type of adultery. Jesus said, "Anyone who even looks at a woman with lust has already committed adultery with her in his heart." Matt 5:28. This can cause great emotional pain in a marriage relationship as well. Pornography is nothing less than looking at another woman with lust. I have seen marriages break up over this.

Maybe one is happy with once a month, once every three months or even once a year or never, but the other wants the sexual union once a day or once or twice a week. You can see there would be some huge compromises on both parts to bring that gap closer together; even then both will be left sacrificing and not totally happy. However, it can be done and it must be done. Remember, we must have self-control and think of the other as well as ourselves. We must compromise to a healthy in-between. But when one is literally suffering through the act so terribly, there is help one can get. Normally both need inner healing when premarital sex has taken place. I have done inner healing sessions with many people and heard wonderful results. Seek help with a trained prayer minister. Not everyone will have these problems, but many do. The prayers already written in this book have helped a lot.

When premarital sex takes place, and even more so when drugs and alcohol or any perversion is involved as well, demons are drawn like flies to decayed flesh. This curses future experiences and needs prayer to purify. Demons can actually occupy the bed with you and your spouse, thus defiling the marriage bed and making it extremely difficult and painful to have intimacy in the marriage bed. It can be felt by one or both, causing a very bad experience. Do not fear! I have seen God do mighty miracles in this area, purifying the marriage bed and returning sex to where He created it to be.

Prayer for Sexual Problems

Both spouses need to humbly repent for every wrong they have done which had to do with sex before marriage; pray from your heart. Repent for every perverse act and the act of the use of drugs during it. Forgive each other. Break the curses that came on you during these acts. Cancel the assignments of the demons and send them away, in the Mighty Name of Jesus. Apply the Blood of Jesus upon you both and upon your bed

and bedroom. The Blood purifies the sin. You may take oil and anoint your bed to purify it, in Jesus' Name.

Both men and women need to repent deeply from the heart for such things that apply, and forgive, and accept forgiveness: **seducing one or others to sex outside of marriage, lust, adultery, homosexual relations, rape, all types of pornography (pornographic magazines, watching perverted movies, Internet pornography, lingerie magazines, idolizing the body or body parts, extra-marital sex with or without spouse's knowledge or permission, peeping toms, overuse of alcohol and drugs, sexual promiscuity, abusive acts during sex, fantasizing about others other than your own spouse, cyber sex, and any other perversions or unspeakable perversions, ungodly, unrighteous, impure acts). All this needs to be dealt with, or will affect, defile and pervert your marriage and marriage bed.**

Maybe it is hard to break from these things, because there is a demon attached that is holding onto you, or to whom you are holding on to. We need to break the demonic bond. It may be controlling you and your weak flesh. After praying, destroy any such materials in your possession. **Renounce each act and the demonic bond of the enemy holding onto you, and break it from you, in Jesus' Name. Loose the bond and cover it with the Precious Blood of Jesus. Do this with each unclean act and partner outside of marriage. Be forgiven, forgive your spouse, forgive yourself and accept God's forgiveness. Also, break the inherited sexual curses carried down from your family line, and the generational spirits of each, in the Mighty Name of Jesus. Break, as well, each ungodly bond with each**

person you were sexually involved with. You can do this alone or best with someone who is anointed, and you will see results.

We must remember that in the sexual relationship there are many different ways we can differ from each other. Different kinds of problems arise where we are unhappy or unfulfilled. We must be open and share our feelings with each other. Often times, when it has to do with sex, we can be very afraid or embarrassed to be open about our feelings, likes, and dislikes. This is especially true if you want to share that you are not being fulfilled by the other, or even feel that you are being hurt by the other. Communication is so important for problems to be resolved. It is hard but well worth it. It is in bringing the issue out in the open that it can be resolved. Often times the other will feel hurt, as if he/she has done something wrong. The ego can get hurt when a spouse feels he or she is not pleasing the other. But it must be gently shared so they realized that it is not always someone's fault. Each individual has special needs. This can be because of personal experiences or body hormonal make up.

You both have to agree on, and enjoy, what is done in your marriage bed. Nothing should ever be negative, painful, perverted, or forced. Don't go into it to only get your own needs met. And don't fantasize about another person; this is sin. Ask, "Am I pleasing you?" "What can I do to make it better for you?" When one shares anything about unhappiness or unfulfillment, the other must care and want to please his/her spouse, and not be offended. Often times one may need extra help being fulfilled – listen, care, and also share where you need help as well. If you are not careful, you can shut the other one down in communicating in this area; it can be difficult for some. No one should ever feel used, shamed, or belittled. The marriage bed should be pure and blessed, because God is present to bless. He created it and it is good. It can be oneness with God and spouse.

Sexual Abuse

Men and women both must realize that "many" women have been sexually abused in one way or another in their lives. This can occur in early childhood or when they are teens and/or in adult life. In fact, it would be a wonderful gesture for a man to vocally ask the woman's forgiveness, standing in for how men in general have mistreated women. You can be specific and stand in for the one who mistreated your wife. If the husband was abused, the woman too can also stand in for the abuser. There is great healing in this. People do not realize that sexual sins do affect the marriage bed.

Inner healing has greater results than just counseling. This is because with inner healing God's healing power actually delivers them, heals the heart, emotions, and even the memory of person. [This type of prayer, where someone stands in for another person, can be done for a variety of reasons. Men can stand in for fathers as well, and women for mothers.] We have seen God perform mighty miracles instantly with this kind of prayer. Often when an incident similar to the abuse happens, the body recalls the memory and it opens the emotional wounds in the woman.[11] It is not only physically painful to the woman but emotionally as well. It can be a similar act that is recreated and the woman may not even remember why she is feeling so bad; she may pull away because the body remembers and subconsciously she remembers.

For example, if a man comes up behind a woman and simply hugs her from behind or touches her in a certain way, it can cause the negative feelings to emerge from the body automatically, causing her to cringe without knowing why.

The man may feel she does not love him, but it has nothing to do with him at all. These are things that can get in the way of a healthy marriage, especially the physical relationship. It can be magnified and very painful. At the same time, it is painful to the husband to feel inadequate, especially when he cannot please her sexually. He can't help but feel it is his fault, even though it has nothing to do with him at all but has everything to do with a past experience. Much of this is not talked about or even understood but is very common in many marriages. Most women, and many men as well, have been sexually abused and/or have had premarital sex these days. This does affect the sexual relationship in marriage. There must be healing by God to bring it to a healthy sexual relationship, even with the one they love with all their heart.

God has set boundaries that keep us in His protection, and premarital sex is outside that boundary. When there is premarital sex, there is a curse that comes, but it can be broken when repented for and prayed for, in Jesus' Name. I have seen it over and over. There is healing for the marriage bed. Seek Christian inner healing or prayer counseling, especially when sexual abuse has taken place. Also if one fears they are homosexual, this kind of counseling has healed many. Sessions with people trained in Elijah House, Theophostic, Healing Streams, or Sozo, are types of good Christian inner healing ministries that work quite well. Seek it out in your city or area churches. Healing can and will come through God. Go through the prayers in the book; they will make a difference.

Breaking all the ungodly soul ties, and breaking all the curses that came upon you because of the sexual act outside of marriage, will help. Most important is forgiving those who hurt you. Breaking the curse off you and breaking the work the enemy did at that time off you, in the Name of Jesus, is also important. Normally there is a lie that is planted at the time of abuse that the woman believes about herself. For example, quite often she may feel it was her fault that she was sexually abused as a young girl; she may feel shame and even be depressed. You can tell her over and over that it was not her fault, but it is not believed until Jesus Himself tells her and brings light to the dark situation. She of course still has memory of it, but Jesus removes the pain.[12]

If you are a husband and your wife has been abused, and you both feel the need to seek help, find a strong credible Christian Prayer Minister, if she is open to it. The same goes for the wife with a husband who has similar problems. It should not be just any counselor but a trained Spirit-filled, anointed prayer minister. Your husband or wife must agree to go. They must understand it will set them free once and for all, and that it will bring great healing to the marriage and the marriage bed.

Keep the marriage bed as pure as you can. This is a way to be ONE with each other and with God at the same time. That is why the enemy has come against sex so strongly to pervert it. Pray beforehand together; pray that God keep it pure. Play anointed worship and/or instrumental worship music, and make it an act of prayer, love, and oneness with God, husband, and wife---one like the Father, Son and Holy Spirit. God created sex, so we know it can be pure and holy because we have a pure and holy God. It does not have to be perverted like the enemy has made it in our society. Many have been so abused that they hate sex and cannot comprehend how God could have created such a terrible thing. That is because they have only experienced the enemy at work to destroy sex as it was created to be. We can learn how God fully intended it to be. Often it takes unlearning the ways of the world and the ways of the enemy. Seek hard after God for His Godly intention for both of you as husband and wife in sexual union, with God's holy presence.

Individual or Group Questions

1. Discuss together how it is going with sexual union?

2. What are my worries or problems with our sexual relationship?

3. How can we improve this area of our relationship?

4. In what ways can we purify our sexual relationship?

5. Do you feel sex is pure and created by God? Why or why not?

12. Spiritual Life

The family that prays together stays together. I remember seeing those words on a billboard years ago. We must keep ourselves strong in the Lord and filled with the Holy Spirit. Remember the parable of the ten virgins in Matthew 25? Five virgins were wise, and five were foolish because they were found empty. We must be found full.   Empty or full of what? Oil. Oil represents the Holy Spirit. How do we stay filled with the Holy Spirit? We stay filled by keeping out of the world's sinfulness as much as possible, by strategically positioning ourselves for the infilling of the Holy Spirit in our lives, and by allowing ourselves to be filled with things of God rather than things of the world, through prayer, worship, reading the Bible regularly, studying the Word together, and soaking in anointed worship. This keeps us cleansed, nourished and strong. If our bodies were left unfed and had no exercise, we would become weak and die of starvation. The same goes with our spirit man. We must feed our spirits regularly and use the spiritual gifts God has given us, or spiritually we will dry up and become dead, as we were before we came to the Lord. It is not sufficient to just read the word; we also need fellowship with other Christians. We need True Worship. "True worshipers will worship the Father in Spirit and Truth. The Father is looking for those who will worship Him that way." John 4:23. It is not enough just to read the word alone; we need to be in a true worshipping church and have fellowship with other believers.

We must also serve the Lord. Jesus said, "My nourishment comes from doing the will of God, who sent me, and from finishing His work." John 4:34. This too helps us to be all He has made us to be. God created us for a purpose, and we must find our call and destiny in the Lord. This is where we will find the most fulfillments in life. When we are fulfilled in the Lord, we will be a blessing to our marriage, our spouse and children, and all those around us by our lives being rich in Him. "Now someone may argue, 'Some people have faith and others have good deeds.' But I say, "How can you show me your faith if you don't have good deeds? I will show you my faith by my good deeds. You say you have faith, for you believe that there is one God. Good for you! Even the demons believe this and they tremble in terror. How foolish! Can't you see that faith without deeds is useless?" James 2:18.

We have had a Healing Rooms Ministry, which is a "drop-in prayer clinic" set outside the church in the community. Most of the people who have come in were born-again Christians who were dried up spiritually. They were born-again Christians who didn't even know if they were born again any longer, meaning they lost all signs of it in their lives. Their churches were not feeding them spiritually, and they came from all different Christian denominations---Catholics to non-denominational and Pentecostals. We would pray for them, and revive them, and teach them how to keep themselves plugged into God. We saw many dried up Christians come back to full life in the Spirit. It really was our biggest work. It is crucial that we get plugged in somewhere, but it has to be a Spirit-Filled Church, whether small in a home or large in a church building. No matter where we are, we should be serving the Lord in some way. Nowhere in the Bible is there a dull spiritual life. Look for it. If you truly are born again, you should be bearing some kind of fruit and showing some signs of spiritual life within you and around you.

We are to be holy as He is holy. Don't be conformed to this world. You can't do it and stay alive in Christ. If you love the world it will hinder your walk. I once saw a young woman's feet firmly planted, one on one side of the fence in darkness and one firmly on the other side in light. There is bound to be a struggle. You can't live on both sides. It is too easy to start believing the lies of the enemy when we flirt with darkness. When we hear the lies of the enemy remember much of it is truth intertwined with lies. I heard it compared to rat poisoning. Rat poisoning is 99% corn. You would think it would be good food but that 1% poison "KILLS" the rat. It is the 1% of deception from the enemy that kills our faith and overcomes the light. Hold on to what you know is true or it will be stolen.

When we are unequally yoked in marriage or even just friendships we become tempted to lose what we know is true. We are tempted to conform to other's beliefs. So befriend like minded believers which even encourage you to be all you can be and to reach your full destiny in Christ. It is too easy to conform to the world when you have a foot in the world. We must hold on to what we know is true. Our truth is altered by darkness if we keep allowing it to infiltrate our thoughts and being. If you continually hang around someone who drinks, takes drugs, steals, or whatever it may be, we lose our shock value and it becomes the norm. We can receive the spirit that is upon them and start making excuses as they do and become "like" them. We begin to believe the lies they do and fall further and further from the truth and not even know it. This is why it is so important to protect yourself and your family from this kind of deception. It can happen to a husband, a wife and most often with our children. When we raise them to be a certain way and they are around the wrong spirit, it is contagious and they begin to believe those who they are around. Suddenly the parent's beliefs seem like foolishness.

Every choice or decision should be brought to God and His direction sought. Nothing is too small or big. Often times women are the spiritual leaders of the family. Most often this has had to be because many men have not taken that rightful place in the home or family. These days though, God is turning that around, and many are coming into their rightful positions. God has shown me that He is calling those now to take their rightful place. Wives need to humble themselves and step aside and allow and even encourage their husbands to take their rightful place as heads of their homes and family. If this is true in your household, the woman needs to step back and allow the man to take his rightful place; this is God's will. This takes dying to self and yielding to the Holy Spirit, even if the woman has led the house for 40 years; she still must step aside, trust God, and let the husband take the lead because this is biblical order for your home. It is a sin if we women prevent the men from taking that rightful place. This is biblical. If you cannot do this then you have issues and have need of healing.

"I want you to understand that the head of every man is Christ, the head of a wife is her husband, and the head of Christ is God." 1 Corinthians 11:3 ESV. "Likewise, husbands, live with your wives in an understanding way, showing honor to the woman as the weaker vessel, since they are heirs with you of the grace of life, so that your prayers may not be hindered." 1 Peter 3:7 ESV.

I am not saying that you won't have input, or that he won't need your help. It is best to lead hand-in-hand together. We were created to be their helpers, because they need us. It is the woman's rightful place to help him. Pray that the men make their choices according to the Holy Spirit. Pray for your husband, be a praying wife, and it will affect your life. Husbands be a praying husband for your wife and children. You can't go wrong when you are praying for each other for God's will. I have seen situations turn around because of prayer. God hears the prayers of the righteous person and answers. Sometimes though, it is not as quickly as we would like.

Find a good, strong, Spirit-filled church or prayer group to get plugged into where you hear the Word, hear good teaching, and receive good strong, intimate, true worship that is spiritually free. This is important for your spiritual growth. Maybe you work on Sundays. Many churches have a weeknight service, and this may be your time rather than Sundays. Find a good Bible Study and make it a priority to go. If there is none to be found, do a Bible Study together in your home. It is important to be strong and not shrivel up and die spiritually. The world is strong, and we must do all we can to stay strong spiritually or the world will try to take us over. If you do this, it will show in your family life and in your attitude and reactions in your family.

It is too easy to fall into sin and not treat your family right. It is hard enough to do what is right when you are with the Lord, let alone when you are dried up and separated from the Lord. Often we don't even know we're dried up. When we're dried up spiritually, we backslide and fall into sin. We need His help and strength; we cannot do it on our own. We are imperfect. That is why we are a husband and wife team and need to be accountable to each other, but not religiously strict as a strict mother or father; this is not right. We are not always strong enough to stay strong by ourselves, especially when we are young or when we are newer in the Lord.

My daughter knew a young man who used to be very strong in the Lord. He separated himself from his church because of hurts, and he began backsliding and did not even know it. She would talk to him and give him scriptures, and he would not receive the truth. This young man thought he was radical in the Lord, but had back slid so far because he disconnected himself from the church and didn't even know it. It is hard when you are hurt, but we must forgive and find a church to get lined up with so we can keep growing. It was hard to believe this young man thought he was ok. Because he was far from God, he was weak and was often falling into sin as a result.

This can happen to any of us. We can think we are ok and everyone can see through you, but you are blinded thinking you are still on track. Others can see the difference where you cannot. If you feel others are judging you because you've changed, instead of getting mad at them look within and see what differences there are from now and before. Have you lined yourself up with wrong people?

We need to make sure we grow, and mature, and reach all God has for us---our fullest potential in Him---reaching our call and our destiny in Him. This goes for individuals as well as couples. He has a call and a purpose for the both of you, individually and as a couple. As Jesus said, "My nourishment comes from doing the will of God who sent me and from finishing His work." John 4:34. We are His mouthpieces, hands, and feet working on earth. Everything in this life is to benefit the Kingdom of God, and our marriage is to benefit God and His will. There is no greater call on earth than to be doing His will and not getting caught up in the cob- webs of the world or getting side tracked. Time is getting short. We are living in the end times now. Jesus said we would see the signs, and we see them now. We need to be doing what Jesus did, not only going to church but Being the Church---not only reading the Word but living the Word, which is His call to every Christian, that the Gospel would be our life, not just Jesus' life. We will do all He did and even greater things we will do.

"I tell you the truth, anyone who believes in me will do the same works I have done and even greater works because I am going to be with the Father. You can ask for anything in My Name and I will do it, so that the Son can bring glory to the Father. Yes, ask me for anything in My Name and I will do it!" John 14:12.

Signs, wonders and miracles should follow every believer. "These miraculous signs will accompany those who believe: They will cast out demons in my Name, and they will speak in new languages. They will be able to handle snakes with safety, and if they drink anything poisonous, it won't hurt them. They will be able to place their hands on the sick and they will be healed." Mark 16:17.

"The Spirit of the Sovereign Lord is upon me, for the Lord has anointed me to bring good news to the poor. He has sent me to comfort the broken hearted and to proclaim that captives will be released and prisoners will be freed. He has sent me to tell those who mourn that the time of the Lord's favor has come." Isaiah 61:1, 2. This was the call of Jesus and should be ours as well.

We cannot pick and choose what to believe out of the Bible. Jesus said anyone who believes in Him will be able to heal, deliver and speak in new languages. Either the Bible is true or Jesus is a liar. We know that Jesus is not a liar, so have the faith to believe what Jesus says. Catch the Holy Spirit in the Word. BELIEVE! If you don't believe, it won't happen for you. It says it happens for those who believe. You merely have to have the faith for it. You get what you have the faith for.

Take advantage of good strong Christian conferences periodically. It helps our growth, especially if we cannot find a good strong church. We really should have a weekly or biweekly worship time in a good church. Our daily spiritual nourishment is up to us. We must discipline ourselves to pray, fast, intercede, worship, take communion often, reading the Bible regularly and soaking before the Lord in anointed music and praying in tongues will strengthen us as well.

Soaking is like a shower in the Holy Spirit, getting cleansed from all the spiritually dirty things that we walk through, see, and are subjected to in this life or on the job, etc. It helps to bring us to our knees, to forgive and ask forgiveness for our wrong doings on a daily basis. Also playing anointed music cleanses our home spiritually and brings peace to our home and those living in it. Praying through our home regularly is needed to cleanse it spiritually, anointing it with oil. Praying through our children's rooms and blessing them, as well as regularly laying hands on them and praying is also cleansing and strengthening for them as well as us. When we stay close to the Lord, and spiritually strong, it really helps our relationship with our spouse and helps us Love more freely. Have your children lay hands on and pray for each other and for you; train them when they are very young. A spiritually strong couple will have a good strong marriage.

Home Family Worship

Hopefully, the man, being the head of the house, will be the spiritual leader and guide his wife and children spiritually. This is not always the case, and many women have had to be the spiritual leaders because the men are not taking the role God has set for them. Leading the family in spiritual things is much like being the pastor of the home. Make sure it is not done "religiously," meaning by actions only and not by the Holy Spirit. Do it all in love and in the power and presence of the Holy Spirit. Don't let home worship practices be dry and empty; God must be present for them to be meaningful, and the Holy Spirit must be present, especially when we are talking about children. Otherwise they will get bored and run from them. Pray for them to be filled with the Holy Spirit and encourage the use of spiritual gifts as taught in 1 Corinthians 12-14.

What do I mean by "religious?" Religion is playing church instead of walking in radical holiness. Religion is living by the law instead of by the Holy Spirit, putting the traditions and rules of man above intimacy with Jesus and passion for Jesus. The Pharisees walked in religion and were prideful of it. They were hard and calloused, and they were set in their ways and unwilling to change. We all carry a certain amount of religious garbage that we grew up with. I know God broke most of that off us through revival. He has to, to enable us to see more of Him. It blinded the Pharisees from even seeing Jesus. It can prevent us from seeing the truth, as well, and prevent our spiritual growth.

We must be flexible to grow closer to God. Jesus always seemed to be breaking the "religious" law. It was the religious that crucified Him, the religious leaders who did not want to change and be flexible in the new ideas preached and walked in by Jesus. They were waiting for a Messiah and thought He was only going to be a certain way, and when He did not fit in that way, they missed Him. Don't miss God in your life because you only think He will be a certain way. Don't shut Him out because He does not fit in your small box and limited way of thinking. He is much bigger and greater, and He will have to stretch you for you to see and experience more of Him and for you to grow.

If you play musical instruments, lead worship with your children in family worship; let them play hand instruments, wave flags and banners, and join in to sing and dance freely. It should always be a fun and joyous experience for them in worshiping God. If you don't play instruments, do the same to good lively worship CDs. Let them play skits from Bible stories for the Word to come alive for them. My children loved this; I made it part of their home school curriculum. Discipline yourselves to worship God regularly from home; don't stop and don't give up, be steadfast.

These are only a few ideas; be creative and think of your own. Ask other spirit-filled parents for their ideas. The main thing is that you want to create a Spirit-filled atmosphere in which they will be able to meet God and worship Him in Spirit and Truth. Don't play church. We want the real thing, God and His True Presence. Begin early in age with them. Lay hands on them and pray for them, allowing them also to lay hands on you and pray for you. They are never too young. Teach them to intercede and pray for each other, for family, the nation, our president and leaders. Let us make sure that as spiritual leaders we show our family love and passion for Jesus, otherwise we are nothing more than a noisy gong. Have times of deep worship. I knew a family who daily had deep musical and spontaneous worship. Their kids were beautiful worshipers!

Make sure you are in a church that really loves the Lord and is passionate for Him and for intimacy with God. Often Jesus is not present, and they don't even notice but keep on playing church. Look for one where God is dwelling; you will find one if you ask God to direct you to where He would have you be. I am very thankful our church is like this; unfortunately, all churches are not like this. Make sure you are being spiritually fed and nourished. Buy teaching CD's and DVD's from powerful conferences, watch God TV, and listen to anointed worship music. Keep yourself filled with the Holy Spirit because the world will not help you with your spirituality. We must feed ourselves physically and this goes for spiritually as well. This undoubtedly will bless your marriage and family. I have known people who said they grew up in praying families, but it was dry and painful and caused them to run *from* God rather than *to* the Lord. Make sure the Holy Spirit is alive in your home prayer. Let your prayer not be just words but deep from your heart. Start when the children are very young. Allow them to lead. Some churches have wonderful youth groups. Not every city has that. It is important that they have strong Christian friends; they become who they spend time with.

Individual or Group Questions

1. Share your favorite scripture with your spouse/fiancé. Read it to them and tell them why it is your favorite. (This tells them something about your spirituality they may not have known before.)

2. Do you feel spiritually alive or dried up? Why?

3. What can we do as a couple to stay stronger and grow? Make a plan.

4. How can we bring God more into our home? Share.

5. Have you been baptized in the Holy Spirit? If doing this in a church setting have leaders and others lay hands for baptism of the Holy Spirit.

5

I am my beloved's and my beloved is mine

"And now I will show you the most excellent way. If I speak in the tongues of men and of angels, but have not love, I am only a resounding gong or a clanging cymbal. If I have the gift of prophecy and can fathom all mysteries and all knowledge, and if I have a faith that can move mountains, give all I possess to the poor and surrender my body to the flames, but have not love, I gain nothing." 1 Corinthians 13:1-3.

Jesus gave us two commandments---to Love God with all our heart and love each other as ourselves. "Love never fails." It is the most excellent way. This is a very important element of "Life." If the Word says it is important, then it is very important. It is the key to ALL that we do. It must be the most important key to marriage. It must be the key to our relationship with God. Scripture shows our relationship with God is like that with our spouse. We can do many wonderful, impressive, important things but without love it all is considered nothing. Without love, everything we do and amount to is nothing. This tells us something important about how our homes should be.

"Love the Lord your God with all your heart, all your soul and with all your strength." Deuteronomy 6:5. This is not easy to do when we did not learn a pure love from our parents. If we did not grow up with love or were not shown a steady love, it is hard for us to keep a passion and steady love for God; but this is how He loves us, steadily and passionately. No matter what we do, either negative or positive, it will not change His unfailing love for us.

"I promised you as a pure bride to one husband, to Christ, NIV says, "so that I might present you as a pure virgin to Him." 2 Corinthians 11:2. He is insinuating that we are the Bride of Christ and we are being presented to our husband, Christ. Understanding the passion of God helps us to be passionate for Him in return and to our husband or wife. When you experience the awesome Love of God, it is easier to love your beloved. When we receive His love, we love them as He loves them. We see beyond the natural.

"...Come and I will show you the bride, the wife of the Lamb. Revelations 21:9. "The Spirit and the bride say, 'Come.'" Rev. 22:17. "Let us be glad and rejoice, and let us give honor to Him. For the time has come for the wedding feast of the Lamb, and His bride has prepared herself." Rev. 19:7.

We "spiritually" are the Bride of the Lamb, and He will have a feast for us and with Him. How glorious that will be! It says we will prepare ourselves. So we have to put effort into preparing ourselves to become spotless, just as Esther did to become prepared for her king; we too are preparing for our King.

Our life is a preparation from the time we are born again and even before we are born again. Jesus put effort into being the sinless Lamb. It did not come easy, but He overcame. We are to overcome. So by loving our beloved we walk the "most excellent way." Let me ask you this important question. How can we stand before the King, Jesus, our Groom, if we did not love or show love for our earthly spouse? What excuse would we have? Put forth effort. Pray for godly love to love the special one God gave you on earth.

When we stay submitted to Christ, we are better husbands and wives. We can't love properly if we don't love God first and put Him first. Stay in unity with God, and then you will have unity of marriage and unity of family. If we are not loving with our family, we are a noisy gong. Think about it; if we do not love each other, we are nothing more than noise. I don't want my prayers to be noise to God.

After many years of marriage, we can tend to take our spouse for granted, get snippy, nag, and even be sarcastic. I pray this convicts your spirit to change, if change is needed. In these end times, we need our voices heard. We must be mouthpieces for God. How can we overcome the difficulties of the world if we cannot overcome our issues with the one who loves us, whom we live with? In order to be productive, we must love.

If we do not love each other as our self, we separate ourselves from God. It is as if we push Him away. Love is the "key" ingredient to a Godly marriage. All else will flow properly. Love forgives a multitude of sins, just by loving. Our walk is not right without it. God does not hear our prayers without it. This is key for our healing. How much authority will we have in saying the prayers in this book, breaking the power of the enemy, if we do not love? It is so important to God that we walk in unity. We can't be one with each other unless we are one with Him. The Holy Spirit is drawn to unity.

Read in the Bible the book Song of Solomon; it is a pattern of how we should have a heart after God and our beloved. It is a book about marriage. It has a natural aspect and a spiritual. It is a love story about Solomon and his wife. But it also is about God and Israel. We are grafted into God's family, so it is a story of us and of God. It is very symbolic and open for interpretation. It teaches us about love. It is about our God and His love for His people...His bride which is us.

"I am my lover's and my lover is mine". Song of Solomon 6:3 "You are so handsome my love, pleasing beyond words." Solomon 1:16. "Let him kiss me with the kisses of his mouth – for your love is more delightful than wine. Pleasing is the fragrance of your perfumes; your name is like perfume poured out." "Take me away with you – let us hurry! Let the king bring me into his chambers." Solomon 1:2.

Loving does not always come natural, nor is it easy, but it has to be worked at. When we experience our God, we receive an abundance of love. To sustain that can be difficult. We must keep ourselves filled spiritually. Most do not stay passionate for God, but it can be done if we work at it. He loves us to be passionate for Him. If you truly catch a glimpse of Him, you will see His passion and love for all mankind. There is no better Lover than our God.

Many Christians are nominal Christians, lukewarm, and they have not experienced the depths of His Love. Yes, I am talking about born again Christians. Yes, even Spirit-filled Christians. There is a depth of His love that is so deep it is endless. Seek Him and you will find Him. If you can get caught up in Him, your life will never be the same. "If you seek the Lord your God, you will find Him if you look for Him with all your heart and with all your soul." Deuteronomy 4:29. "As the deer pants for streams of water, so my soul pants for you, O God. My soul thirsts for God, for the living God. When can I go and meet with God?" Psalm 42:1-2.

Know this; wherever you are with God, you can go much further. Also, regardless of what you have done for Him so far, you can do so much more and He's calling you to more. When you experience the depths of His Love, you want to do more out of your passion, thankfulness and love that you have for Him. The same goes for your earthly beloved. You must work to sustain the love and passion you began with before marriage and as newlyweds. We don't want to just sustain it, but we want it to grow through the years. Make your marriage a priority. By ignoring your husband, wife or marriage, it will fizzle away and you may have a nominal marriage. Many have enough love to get by; many don't even have that.

The enemy is causing so many to divorce, you cannot get by on "nominal," or mediocre in your marriage or with the Lord. Times are getting harder; tough trials are coming for us all. God wants us tight with our marriage. I feel that is why God is having me write this book. Lukewarm in our marriage or in our relationship with God will never get us through. Jesus said that He will spit you out of his mouth if you are found lukewarm with Him. Neither should your marriage be lukewarm. Keep the love and passion alive by keeping God's love and passion alive. We need to be strong with each other and the Lord, because the days are getting darker with a lot more immorality. We need each other to stand strong. We're a team. That is where the enemy will attack---be aware!

"I am my beloveds and my beloved is mine." Solomon 6:3. He will teach you all you need about Love. For He is Love! As we draw close to Him and experience His love, He expands our ability to love; loving Him, our husband, wife, our children, and our neighbors. There is no other way for us to know how to truly love without His love first, unconditional love. Let us always be mindful of where we began as a couple, and how we began. Stay in touch with your first love. Jesus! "We love because He loved us first." 1 John 4:19 ESV.

"I have told you these things so that you will be filled with my joy. Yes, your joy will overflow! This is my commandment, Love each other in the same way I have loved you. There is no greater love than to lay down one's life for one's friends." John 15:11.

"God's Love endures forever!" Palm 136:2.

"For God loved the world so much that He gave His one and only Son, so that everyone who believes in Him will not perish but have eternal life." John 3:16.

We can work at having a Godly marriage to put this book into practice, but the Holy Spirit is the one who does the work in us and through us. Know it is done by yielding yourselves to God. God Bless you and your marriage! I pray the Holy Spirit works in your hearts and teaches you the secrets of His Spirit.

If you do not know Jesus as your personal friend and Savior or do not have the infilling of the Holy Spirit, recite this prayer:

Dear Jesus, I thank you for dying for me on the cross. I acknowledge my sins, and I am very sorry for my sins. Please forgive me and cleanse me of all my sins. Come into my heart and live in me. Help me. I need you in my life. I accept you into my

heart this day. Fill me with Your Holy Spirit. Change my life, and make me new. In Jesus' Name, I pray.

Please recite this prayer. It is the very prayer that changed my life and my husband's life over thirty years ago. Recite it daily.

**Come Holy Spirit;
Fill the hearts of your faithful.
Enkindle in us the fire of Your Love.**

**Send forth Your Spirit,
and we shall be created,
and you shall renew the face of the earth.**

Epilogue

Communicating Feelings

Writing Exercise

Here are some questions you might ask one another. This will help you and your spouse to understand each other, and why you might be different now that you're married than you were before when you were dating. It should help you to do the things that are important to your mate. First separate in different rooms, and then write your feelings to all the questions in #1 on paper or in a notebook. Come together, switch papers and go back alone in a room to read what the other has written. Then after reading, come together and discuss. Sometimes writing questions or problems helps. Some people send e-mails to discuss before facing it in person. Sometimes when it is a difficult issue that is hard to share, writing a letter is the easiest way.

Answer the next questions in #2. You can do this at the same time or the next day. Come together and exchange to read each other's feelings. Then come together and discuss face to face.

Questions like these may be answered more honestly and more completely if done on paper. This will also help you understand your own feelings. First is Married Couples Questions and below that is Engaged Couples Questions.

Married Couples Questions

1. a) What is different now that we are married than when we were dating? Things that I did not expect to change? How does that makes me feel? b) Name specifically what is different that the other is doing or not doing? c) Why it is important to me? d) How does that make me feel? Exchange answers and read each other's answers in separate rooms, then answer the next question in your notebook or on your paper. Use as much paper as needed. Answer fully your feelings. Do this exercise according to the time you have. Do one or two questions at a time.

2. a) How does it make me feel to hear what my wife/husband said? b) Why am I doing these things differently now? b) Am I able to do these again since they are important to my spouse? c) Why or why not? (It could be critical to saving the marriage.) Exchange notebooks or papers and go into separate rooms to read when you both are finished writing.

Next: Come together to discuss thoroughly, hug and kiss! This may be very stressful, but it is important to come to an understanding on these issues if there are any issues. Try to feel your spouse's feelings. It should matter to you.

On another day, answer these next questions on paper in separate rooms. Answer both questions and then read each other's answers.

1. a) Marriage is better or worse than I thought it would be? Why? Answer the next question

2. a) Am I happy? b) Am I struggling? Why or why not? b) How happy am I on a scale of 1 – 10. The reason?

Exchange and read each other's. Come together and discuss. After discussion, answer the last question.

3. a) How did that discussion make me feel? b) How does it make me feel (if) my spouse is hurting or not happy or is happy? c) What can I do to be a better husband or wife to help my marriage be a happy one?

It is important to answer and resolve these difficulties which could eventually lead to deeper trouble in the marriage. If these issues are unresolved and cause the marriage to end, your issues could lead to another unhappy marriage. Deal with them now and strengthen this marriage.

Next Day: Write again. Then exchange papers or notebooks.

1. a) What qualities do I love about my spouse? b) What things do I love about what you are doing in our marriage? Exchange and read each other's answers. Come together and discuss your feelings.

Next Day:
1) a) What do I love most about you right now?
b) What do I love about our marriage?
c) How does that make me feel?

2) a) What am I having a problem dealing with in

197

our relationship? How does that make me feel?

b) How does this make me feel?

c) How can we solve this?

Hopefully, this exercise will help the other one to understand yourself and your spouse better. Whether married a short time or a long time, you will benefit from this. You might even start a notebook/journal to write things to each other to keep the communication going, if this helps. Choose some topics to share about. If you are engaged, get these questions out a couple of months after you are married and answer them.

ENGAGED QUESTIONS

If you are engaged, you can do this as well with different questions. 1a.) List things I like about our relationship. b) I like it when you...and how does this make me feel? c) I hope these things continue when we get married...list. d) Why do I hope they continue? e) What I hope does NOT continue after we get married.

Exchange notebooks to read. Then answer the next question.

2.) How does that make me feel? a) Where do I agree or disagree? b) I don't think I would continue these things...list...because...tell them why you would not want to continue. And these I would love to continue.

Exchange and read. Come together and discuss.

Next Day:

1) List things that could be better in our relationship. I don't like it when you... Exchange answers to read and then answer the next question. a) How does this make me feel? Read and then come together to discuss. Go on to the next question.

2) When we are married, I envision it to be like this... List your expectations of each other and married life.

Exchange and read. Write in your notebook how this makes you feel. Bring together to discuss. Discussions are good and help you to get to know each other's wants, needs and expectations better.

Look up love language test and find out how your spouse expects to be loved and how he/she gives it. Make sure as an engaged couple you go to some kind of pre-marriage program. Not only will it be fun, but it is there to help prevent divorce. Don't skip it! It will help you get to know each other better.

Do I view marriage as an escape from something?

Be sure to take advantage of premarital programs your church may have.

Be sure to take the compatibility test to confirm your compatibility.

ENDNOTES

[1] Elijah School for Prayer Ministry Basic 1 Ministry Training by John and Paula Sandford

[2] Paul Cox's Discernment Course. Aslan's Place Hesperia, CA 92345

[3] Elijah House School for Prayer Ministry Basic 1 Ministry Training by John and Paula Sandford.

[4] Elijah School for Prayer Ministry Basic 1 Ministry Training by John and Paula Sandford.

[5] Dr. John Gray, Men are from Mars Women are from Venus 1992 Harper Collins Publishers

[6] Mary Baxter Divine Revelation of Hell Whitikar House Publishers New Kensington, PA

[7] Webster's Collegiate Dictionary G & C Merriam Co. 1979

[8] Webster's Collegiate Dictionary G & C Merriam Co. 1979

[9] Webster's Collegiate Dictionary G & C Merriam Co. 1979

[10] Fireproof 2008 Ryko Distribution Directed by Alex Kendrick

[11] Ed M. Smith Beyond Tolerable Recovery Alathia Publishing P.O. Box 489 Campbellsville, Kentucky 42719

[12] Ed M. Smith Beyond Tolerable Recovery Alathia Publishing P.O. Box 489 Campbellsville, Kentucky 42719

About the Author

Diane and her husband have been married for over 36 years. They have two daughters, a son and a son in law. They also have three wonderful grandchildren. They are from upstate New York and now reside in Branson, Missouri. They have been leaders in the Christian Community for over 30 years and are Ordained Ministers and founders of Restore the Glory Ministries. They led Charismatic and Revival Prayer meetings for over 20 years and also pastored a small church. They founded Binghamton Healing Rooms in New York State. Diane also has training and experience in Healing, Inner Healing, and Deliverance Ministry. She has done Pastoral Counseling and Prayer Counseling Ministry. She has taught on healing, biblical dream interpretation, and the prophetic. She wrote and taught for a revival newsletter. Author of "His Body, His Blood". More info: www.RestoreTheGloryMinistries.com

Books by Author
Diane Czekala

Keys to a Godly Marriage
For Married and Engaged Couples
Includes Prayers for Healing, Deliverance and Breaking Curses

His Body, His Blood
More to Communion than Meets the Eye

To see these and others coming go to:
www.RestoreTheGloryMinistries.com

6600391R0

Made in the USA
Charleston, SC
11 November 2010